RICHARD ASHCROFT
THE VERVE, BURNING MONEY & THE HUMAN CONDITION

Published in 2008 by
INDEPENDENT MUSIC PRESS
Independent Music Press is an imprint of I.M. P. Publishing Limited
This Work is Copyright © I. M. P. Publishing Ltd 2008

Richard Ashcroft – The Verve, Burning Money & The Human Condition
by Trevor Baker

British Library Cataloguing-in-Publication Data.
A catalogue for this book is available from The British Library.
ISBN: 978-1-906191-02-3 & 1-906191-02-6

Cover Design by Fresh Lemon.
Cover photograph by Steve Double/Retna

Printed in the UK.

Independent Music Press
P.O. Box 69,
Church Stretton, Shropshire
SY6 6WZ
Visit us on the web at: www.impbooks.com
and www.myspace.com/independentmusicpress
For a free catalogue, e-mail us at: info@impbooks.com
Fax: 01694 720049

Richard Ashcroft

The Verve, Burning Money

& The Human Condition

by Trevor Baker

Independent Music Press

ACKNOWLEDGEMENTS

Thanks to everybody who kindly agreed to be interviewed for this book: John Best, Brian Cannon, Derek Chapman, Simon Clarke, BJ Cole, Miles Leonard, Roger Morton, Tim Sanders, Phill Savidge, Ajay Sharma and Michael Spencer Jones. Also all the Richard Ashcroft and Verve websites, in particular www.the-verve.info, whose interview with Chris Potter was particularly useful and www.musicsaves.org/verve and www.astorminheaven.com for their comprehensive news and press sections. Other websites without which this book would have been much harder to write include http://thevervelive.blogspot.com, www.theverveunofficial.com and www.richardashcroftonline.com. The book wouldn't have been possible without all the interviews conducted by various journalists for magazines, radio and TV over the years. Thanks, in particular, to Martin Aston and Andrew Smith for invaluable details of Richard's childhood featured in their early Nineties articles for *Select* and *Melody Maker* magazines. Thanks also to Darren Taylor for permission to use the transcript of his excellent 2000 interview with Richard Ashcroft.

CONTENTS

INTRODUCTION

On the flattened grass at the back of Hyde Park, Richard Ashcroft sits, leaning against a Portakabin, drinking a bottle of beer and puffing nervously on a cigarette. From inside the cabin, he can hear Coldplay practising their scales. A little further away there's the sound of thousands of people streaming across the grass towards the stage for Live 8 – the biggest gig of the year, where, in just a few hours, he'll be singing his biggest song. As he listens to the band he wonders idly whether maybe it should be him practising his scales, since he's the one who'll be doing most of the singing.

"I'm thinking, that's where it all went wrong," he joked to *The Telegraph* afterwards. "I'm smoking a cigarette and I'm singing the whole fucker myself!"

Things have changed, in other words, since his old band, Verve, as they were then called, prepared for their first London gig by "getting wasted in the park." In 2005 he'd been solo for six years since The Verve split up for the second acrimonious time. "80% of that time," he once said, "was depressing." At Live 8 he was as much a symbol of a different era as Pink Floyd who would play later. A rock star stranded in an era that didn't really do stars anymore.

Was that the moment when he first started to toy with the idea of reforming The Verve? He'd vociferously deny it for two more years but there must have come a point when he wondered if he could ever recreate on his own the inexplicable magic of being in a band.

In 1989, when his band had started, there were no real stars, either. In Manchester, Ian Brown and Shaun Ryder were re-inventing the concept of the frontman as shaman. Elsewhere guitar music was dominated by acts who scorned charisma as a cheap trick. Verve's first singles baffled and enthralled in equal measure and their live shows were jaw-droppingly good. They made a brilliant and underrated debut album but were then quickly overtaken in the commercial stakes by bands like Suede, Blur and, later, Oasis who were prepared to write classic three minute pop songs.

They began to talk about something they called the 'Verve voodoo' which brought them low every time it looked like they might take off. There were broken bones, relationship break-ups, backstage collapses, legal problems, drug use and, not once but twice, the break-up of the band itself.

Out of all this chaos came some of the best loved songs of the Nineties. The first real sign of their breakthrough came with 'History', written by Richard when he was still reeling from a painful split with the girlfriend he'd had since his teens. It looked like giving them everything they'd ever wanted – massive success twinned with credibility. Instead the pure excess of the recording sessions for the accompanying album, *A Northern Soul*, almost destroyed them. Guitarist Nick McCabe recoiled from the pressure and Richard pulled the plug.

They got back together and Richard revealed two songs he'd written that would change everything: 'Bitter Sweet Symphony' and 'The Drugs Don't Work'. They turned him from an indie icon into a 'celebrity'. This in a time just before 'celebrity' merely meant somebody who'd been in a reality TV show.

Absurdly The Verve were now viewed by the tabloids as exciting late arrivals to the glamorous Britpop scene. Richard's marriage of two years to ex-Spiritualized keyboard player Kate Radley was reinvented in the press as a celebrity affair. The band really had got everything they wanted and yet it seemed this could be a stark lesson in 'being careful what you wish for'.

In 1999, Richard pulled the plug again. Apparently for good. Being in The Verve had never been easy. His first solo hit, 'A Song For The Lovers', came from the same batch of songs as 'Bitter Sweet Symphony' and 'The Drugs Don't Work'. He'd envisioned all three as the first songs of his solo career – maybe he should have stuck with his original plan?

But something was wrong. He'd never really *loved* playing on his own. He missed the chaos of being in a band. His first solo album, *Alone With Everybody*, did reasonably well but it sold a fraction of the number of copies of *Urban Hymns*. His second solo album, *Human Conditions*, sold even less than its predecessor. By Live 8, he was about to release a third solo album, *Keys To The World*, but even then he wasn't certain to carry on solo.

Maybe being on stage in front of 200,000 people reminded him of what The Verve had achieved and what they could have achieved. Not long afterwards, reports suggested he was suffering from depression. In 2006, staff at a Wiltshire youth centre called the police after he turned up demanding to be allowed to help the kids and refusing to leave. The story took yet another twist.

In 2007 the inevitable happened. Hatchets were buried for the third time and Richard announced that The Verve were getting back together – a deeply misunderstood group, fighting to reclaim their legacy. Were they the pop band of classic songs like 'Sonnet' and 'Lucky Man' or were they the avant-guard psychedelic rock band of their early singles? Did they sell-out by writing tunes that sold a million or did they finally live up to their potential?

This book is an attempt to answer those questions and to tell the story of an outwardly super-confident artist with a wilfully introspective and complex streak. From the first flowering of Richard's drive and ambition as a young child, to the current third coming of The Verve, this story takes in every stumble and every triumph. Maybe this time around, The Verve will be the biggest band in the world, as they once promised. Or maybe they'll bitterly implode once more.

To this day, it's always seemed impossible for The Verve to stay together, but it's equally impossible for them to stay apart. Ashcroft's role in that – and his own complicated and fascinating life and career – is one of modern rock's most compelling tales.

CHAPTER 1

THE ROAD FROM WIGAN PIER

When Richard Ashcroft was 11 years old, his dad died. It might seem like a biographical cliché to say that that was the moment everything changed but there's some truth in it. With his mother still at the hospital, he was taken to stay at his friend's house, the son of a vicar. Struggling for something to say, the friend tried to comfort him by talking about God and the afterlife but Richard wasn't listening. "I remember thinking, 'Right, religion's out from this day on,'" he would later tell Andrew Smith of *Melody Maker*.

He had a furious argument with his friend. He couldn't understand how, if there's a loving God, somebody could be there one minute and gone the next. His dad, Frank, had been in a car crash many years before and it left him with a tiny blood clot in his brain which, in 1982, haemorrhaged and killed him. Frank had often been unwell for the last few years of his life but there was no indication that he could die so suddenly. It left Richard with relatively few memories of his father. All he remembered was a man with the same prominent nose as him and the same wide mouth. He remembered a man who'd loved to be the centre of attention but who'd spent his life working hard from nine-to-five and then suddenly had that all taken away.

The shock gave Richard an overpowering sense of the fragility of existence. It also gave him what he later described as something close to a "narcissistic disorder" – a compulsive desire for love and acclaim. "There was a big feeling that I was going to be up to something in my life, you know?" he said many years later in an interview with Michael Devereaux of *Filter* Magazine. "I hadn't quite figured out what it was, but I had that sort of urgency that other people didn't seem to have at the time. Whether that was being a rock star ... I don't know."

It's relatively common for successful people to have suffered this kind of loss. According to psychologist Oliver James, the drive to succeed that's found in everybody from world leaders to self-made millionaires is often a way of dealing with something missing.

"Exceptional achievers are determined to wrest their destiny from fickle fate through impregnable success," he wrote in *The Times*, "never again to be at its mercy, as they were when the parent died."

Oliver James was talking about American presidents or about political leaders but it might not be stretching the theory too much to apply the same analysis to Richard. He clearly got his incredible drive from somewhere. Initially he dealt with the loss – he said – by "swallowing it". In the weeks after Frank's death, other people tried to comfort him but he pushed them away. Well-meaning local fathers offered to take him out, to take his mind off things, but it didn't help.

"I got taken on a lot of boat trips," he said to website *Mr Beller's Neighborhood*. "These other dad's were doing it because my dad had died, and after three depressing trips on the boat you finally say to your mum, 'Look, make sure they don't take me on the boat again because the boat is making me more depressed!'"

His only visible response to the bereavement was to take refuge in music. After John Lennon had died, just over a year before, he'd played 'Imagine' repeatedly. The first record he ever bought was 'Just Like Starting Over'. His mother, hairdresser Margaret, was quick to encourage his interest. He says his family only had five albums – The Beatles *Revolver*, Northern Soul compilation *Black Explosion*, Pink Floyd's *The Final Cut*, a Carpenters record and another by the Stylistics – but he supplemented his own music collection by obsessively taping songs off the radio.

From being a relatively content, if sickly child (he was told at the age of five that he'd have a cold for the rest of his life), he started taking certain drugs in his late teens. It suited both sides of his character, the energetic fun-seeker and the introspective dreamer who just liked to get stoned and think about the meaning of life.

Even before his dad died, he was always a dreamer. His grandfather, who owned a telescope, used to take him to look at the stars and make him think about the vastness of the universe and the insignificance of the Earth "spinning silently", as he'd later put it, in space. At school his "narcissistic disorder" manifested itself in a need to constantly be the centre of attention and make the other kids laugh.

There were few remaining traces of the shyness that had once led to him being "sacked" from the nativity play ("I was shaking so much," he said in an interview with *The Guardian*, "Terrible nervous guy.") One teacher even dubbed him "the cancer of the class" – a jibe which still hurt years later.

It was a difficult time anyway, not just for Margaret, her son and two younger daughters Victoria and Laura, but for much of the country. The early Eighties were tough for northern England, and their home town of Wigan was no exception. For a long time, the town was best known as the subject of George Orwell's *The Road To Wigan Pier* – an exposé of poverty in the working classes. Things were better in the Eighties, but not all that much. The once successful textiles industry was on the rocks, the last of its mills closed in 1980, and many people worked for food manufacturer Heinz at their massive factory.

Even when it was part of the North West's industrial boom, Wigan was always overshadowed by its more famous neighbours Liverpool and Manchester. Musically it hadn't produced any real stars since George Formby in the Thirties, although it had a claim to fame as the spiritual home of Northern Soul music. Its most famous club, the Wigan Casino, was once voted "the world's best discotheque" and at its peak many thousands of people visited to dance to obscure American soul records from labels like Motown, Stax and many smaller independents. Because of this the music scene in the area was often more heavily influenced by what was going on in places like Detroit and Chicago than London or the rest of the south of England.

But the Wigan Casino closed down in 1981 and the whole of the North West was in an economically depressed state. The most significant band from the region (rather than Wigan itself) at the start of the Eighties was Joy Division, playing music that could only come from a depressed, post-industrial area. Unemployment was high and Richard's mother Margaret had to bring up the whole family on the money she made from hairdressing. At the age of twelve, like so many other kids, Richard became a huge fan of The Smiths, another band who could only have come from the North West.

"An older friend got into The Smiths," he said in a video interview with *Planet Rock*. "I remember getting *Hatful Of Hollow* and playing 'How Soon Is Now?' on headphones and getting into that teen angst period. Johnny Marr's guitar was a defining moment. I was wondering why this music was having such an effect on me."

He could have become the stereotypical Morrissey-worshipper – sitting in a darkened bedroom wallowing in misery. In the end, though, his innate energy and enthusiasm meant that moping wasn't really an option. "I was starting to go out and have fun and discover girls at this time," he told *Melody Maker*. "This was everything Morrissey was meant to be against, but I just didn't want to take him that seriously."

Despite this comment, he already had the typical rock star's mixture of insecurity and self-confidence, an extrovert desire to be noticed and an accompanying tendency towards introspection. As he got older, Richard even took advantage of his mother's profession – cajoling her into regularly changing his haircut. Later, after he became famous, a schoolfriend, Michael Newton, told *The Sun* that his nickname was 'Jesus' because of his constant desire for attention.

Despite his slim frame, he also had a tendency to get into fights. On his first day at school, he got into an argument with another kid. By the end of the day, they were standing on opposite ends of the playground, lining up with their mates and hurling abuse at each other. This was highly uncharacteristic for the other kid. He was Pete Salisbury – nicknamed 'Sobbo' – a man whom, it would later be said, "didn't have a bad bone in his body". Pete was born in Bath in the South West but he lived near Richard in Up Holland. As the drummer, first in The Verve and then with Richard Ashcroft's solo band, he would be stuck with his playground antagonist for at least the next 25 years. As Joy Division bassist Peter Hook once said of his long love-hate relationship with vocalist Bernard Sumner "you get less time for murder."

A little while later, Richard also met another kid who'd recently moved into the area – Simon Jones, later to be The Verve's bass player. Simon grew up in Liverpool where he was born but at the age of thirteen he enrolled at Up Holland High, too.

Arguably it was Richard's furious desire to make something of himself that changed all of their lives. Simon once recalled asking the fourteen-year-old Richard what he was going to do when he grew up. Richard replied that he was going to be the singer in a band. "I'm going, 'Yeah, yeah, yeah,' Simon told website *Exclaim!* later. "We couldn't even fucking play a note."

Part of Richard's confidence and self-belief may have come from a feeling that he had to rely on himself but he also had a new source of guidance by then. After his dad died, his mother later married a teacher called Doug Ashcroft, a follower of the principles of the Rosicrucian order – a seventeenth century religious group who believed in the power of mind over matter. Most famously they believed in creative visualisation – the idea that you could make something happen by visualising it. This was a belief that would have a huge impact on Richard's later life. Although he ultimately rejected all forms of organised religion, at fourteen he even decided that he was a Rosicrucian himself.

Before he wanted to be a singer, though, he thought that he would make his mark as a footballer. He might have made it, too. He was considered a good prospect, he played for Up Holland Boys and even attended the famous Bobby Charlton Soccer School. Unfortunately, the discipline and strict training regimes didn't always agree with him – he was too busy dreaming about being the next George Best. In reality, football in the late Eighties wasn't all that glamorous. There were similarities with the rock scene. It was a dour period dominated by talk of "the grid system" and playing the percentages. There was little room for individual flair. Richard got sent off on more than one occasion, often for talking back to the referee, and he had his nose broken four times. At one point he also broke Sobbo's leg with a particularly ferocious tackle. Ultimately, he says, the manager of Up Holland FC made him "hang up his boots" and, realising that he was never going to be as good as his heroes anyway, he decided to turn his attention elsewhere.

"I wouldn't mind being that guy who scores the winning goal in the Cup Final," he told *Melody Maker* in 1992, "but I know that come Monday morning that guy's got to be up at seven and running round a field."

At the start of his teens, something new came into his life. When he was thirteen he went on a camping trip and the nearby youth centre had a TV that, one night, his group of friends were allowed to stay up late and watch. "For some mad reason, the regional TV showed that Godard film, *One Plus One*," he told US magazine *Mean*. "I saw this and immediately went, 'That's the way to spend your life.'"

One Plus One was the rarely seen film that French director Jean-Luc Godard made with the Rolling Stones in the late Sixties. It showed a life of debauchery, decadence and freedom that was a huge contrast with the rigorous discipline of Eighties football and life in Wigan. More importantly it also showed, in detail, the creation of a great song – 'Sympathy For The Devil'.

That year on holiday in Cornwall, Richard supposedly told people, "You better remember me – you better remember Richard Ashcroft." It wasn't the beginning of his belief that he was destined for great things – that burning desire had been there for years already – but he had started to conceive a more concrete idea about how he was going to get there.

As he got grew through his teens, he started to delve deeper and deeper into music and the counterculture that went with it. When his parents moved away to the Cotswolds, Richard moved into his first flat with friend Wayne Griggs who was later to be a successful DJ with The Verve and others. Wayne already had an incredible music collection which was bolstered by his dad's love of soul. Richard would later describe Wayne and people like him as "the hunters". They were the people who foraged through stacks of vinyl in record shops looking for the best new music and those elusive lost classics.

Wayne would bring new records home by relatively obscure artists and, initially, Richard would always claim to be highly unimpressed. "I'd always laugh at whatever he got, even if I knew it was fantastic," he said later. At this point he started vaguely thinking about making his own music but didn't yet know how to play any instruments. It wasn't until Richard, Sobbo and Simon Jones went to Winstanley College to do their A-levels that forming a band started to seem realistic. Even more so when they got to know another student, Simon Tong.

Simon had been at the same secondary school, but at Winstanley they got to know him better and discovered that he could play the guitar. He taught both Richard and Simon their first chords.

Another guitarist, however, was to have an even greater influence. It was at Winstanley that Richard first heard a sound coming out of a college practise room which he was to describe as "a whole other universe to me." The door to the room was shut so Richard just waited outside.

"I didn't know what he looked like," he said to *Planet Rock* later, "so I just waited for whoever was making that noise to come out." Eventually the student, Nick McCabe, stopped playing, unplugged his guitar and got ready to go home but, as he walked outside, was confronted with Richard Ashcroft who stopped him and said: "I want to be in a band with you."

CHAPTER 2

VERVE

Nick McCabe was in the year above Ashcroft at Winstanley. He was quieter and more introspective but there was an aura about him at school because one of his brothers, Paul, was something of a local tearaway. "He was in prison by the time he was fourteen," Nick told *Select* magazine. "He ran away from home – stole three cars to get to Birmingham and was being chased by Range Rovers down the M6."

Nick was the polar opposite to Richard in some respects. He hadn't got into music to make the world notice him. He didn't particularly welcome attention. He just liked creating sounds for their own sake. He wasn't even interested in being the traditional guitar hero with the complete mastery of chords and guitar solos. Instead, the guitar was just an instrument like any other, to be manipulated and taken to its limits.

At college it was much easier to find other like-minded music fans than it had been at school. Sobbo immediately began drumming in a marching band and then a group called The Comedians, while Simon Jones and Simon Tong formed a band that was known as Laughing Gravy and then Applecart.

Richard was desperate to join in but he still didn't have an instrument. Eventually his mum caved in, took a train to Liverpool and bought him his first guitar in the shop where John Lennon had famously bought his. It was probably a sign of the times that there was nowhere in the whole of Wigan where you could buy a decent guitar.

Richard immediately formed his first band with Nick McCabe and another friend on bass. At that point they didn't have a drummer, just a drum machine, and Nick wasn't keen to be stuck on the guitar all the time. He'd always loved the possibilities presented by electronic music. This was a time when rock wasn't fashionable at all. Grunge was still deep underground in America and critically acclaimed British rock bands such as My Bloody Valentine sold in tiny quantities. Suddenly DJs were emerging as superstars and in the music press the new cliché was for guitar bands to claim that "there's always been a dance element to our music". At the same time, hip-hop was starting to have a major impact in the UK for the first time and bands like Public Enemy and De La Soul were considered far more cutting edge than any group with a guitar. Clubbing appeared to be the future. The mainstream of music in the mid-to-late Eighties had little or nothing to offer Richard.

"Back in the Eighties, whenever you turned on the TV it was Phil Collins, it was Robert Palmer, it was Peter-fucking-Gabriel," Richard said to *Time Out* magazine, "all these people who were in something before you were conscious! It was like, 'who are these geezers with suits on who keep getting hits, Mum?'"

Then Richard saw the Stone Roses for the first time. "Seeing them play Warrington in 1989 basically changed my life," he told Martin Aston of *Select*. "These guys looked and dressed like me and they were from the same background, yet they were on-stage, being adored. Seeing them made me realise that I could do that as well. I could do better."

Suddenly it was cool to be in a traditional four-piece rock band again, without necessarily having to make traditional four-piece rock music. And, what was more, the centre of the universe was just down the road in Manchester. Manchester had changed dramatically since the arrival of ecstasy a few years before. In the past it had been renowned for music which was as bleak as its weather. Its most famous club, the Haçienda, had always played some indie music and The Smiths and Joy Division were untouchable icons – as were New Order, who part-owned the venue. The club was famously dance-orientated and, by 1987, DJ Mike Pickering was hosting a hugely popular dance music night.

Dance music seeped into almost everything. The Stone Roses, who'd been vaguely gothic Byrds fans, suddenly discovered a groove, while the Happy Mondays' version of rock was pilled-up, beat-strewn and chaotic. By 1989 the music press had coined the term 'Madchester' (others say Factory Records did) and the whole

North West was buzzing. On one famous edition of *Top Of The Pops*, the two bands appeared together and, for the first time, Manchester wasn't just the home to cool artists, it was a cool place in itself. Suddenly the student population rocketed as thousands of eighteen-year-olds wanted to move there and the downtrodden, post-industrial town had a new spring in its step.

Nick might have wanted to go in a more electronic direction too, but Richard had other ideas. He was a huge fan of Nick's instinctive, unorthodox guitar style and he would have loved to be able to play like that. Their first band, known as The Butterfly Effect and then Raingarden, was based mostly around Nick's guitar and Richard's vocals. They began playing in the canteen of Winstanley and that's where the famed 'Mad Richard' persona of later years was first formed as, to the astonishment of the other students, he threw himself on to the floor and began rolling around as Nick carried on playing. At that point, it was the only way he felt he could express anything like the same intensity and energy as Nick's playing.

"These kids were just staring at me, going, 'What a wanker – what the fuck is he doing?' Richard said to *Select* magazine. "My friends thought I'd cracked. But I just couldn't help it."

At the time, hundreds of new bands were emerging, many of them with the stereotypical 'dance element' to their sound. By then, Richard was living with Simon Jones in Wigan. Simon was still playing relatively rudimentary bass but, as their exams got closer, Richard encouraged him and Pete Salisbury to join them. Now a four-piece, they called themselves 'Verve'.

So far they'd managed to avoid getting thrown out of Winstanley but they'd been spending much of their time sitting on the nearby hills, drinking in abandoned cars. Now, though, they began practising, jamming furiously to try and find a sound. There was no likelihood that Verve would simply leap on-board the nearest bandwagon. They loved the Stone Roses but they also loved Led Zeppelin and numerous other, less hip, bands. Unlike many kids of their age, they'd collectively been exposed to a huge amount of music, not just what was happening around them. They loved slow, trippy sounds rather than the frantic beat of dance and this was the kind of music they wanted to make.

Music was starting to take over Richard's life and it was becoming increasingly clear that if he couldn't make a career out of it, then academia was probably not going to offer an easy alternative either. Later on he remembered the first time he told teachers that he was going to be a musician. "I got the classic wry smile that said, 'You're gonna be working in a factory in two years, son.'" he said to *Melody Maker*. That prediction looked like it might have been coming true when he suffered poor results in his exams.

One day he was sat in his Philosophy and Religion A-Level exam, the sun was shining outside and he simply thought 'What am I doing here?' then got up and left. His teachers were so worried that they actually contemplated dragging the canals. He was offered counselling but declined. Although later he might claim that his success was inevitable, it didn't seem like it at the time. When he left college, while Sobbo went to do a ceramics course in Stoke and Nick became a trainee quantity surveyor in Liverpool, Richard went straight on the dole. He would only ever had one 'proper' job in his life. When he told the careers adviser at school that he wanted to be a rock star, the teacher was, unsurprisingly, dubious.

"'What's the band called?' he asked. '"I don't know', Richard replied. 'Can you play?' 'No.' 'Have you got any songs?' 'No.' 'Have you got any ideas?' 'No. But that's what I'm going to do."

The careers adviser quickly scanned down his list of options for the nearest equivalent to 'rock star' and suggested that Richard become a lifeguard. For the time being it would have to do. At least the idea of being a heroic life-saver appealed to him. When he got there, though, it was quickly discovered that he didn't have the appropriate swimming badges. So they set him on to cleaning the toilets. He barely lasted a week before going back on the dole.

In a verse from the song 'History', he'd later sing about an epiphany, sitting on a hillside above Wigan with Simon Jones, looking at all the people below. "Looking at all the lights," he explained to Stuart Maconie in a *Q* interview, "I thought to myself that out of those millions of lights, not one of them knows me and we're just fucking rotting away on the dole doing nothing. That was the first spark."

Verve played their first gig at a birthday party for Richard's friend Paul Frodsham at the Honeysuckle pub in Wigan in 1989. They only had two songs but they were good enough to inspire another friend, Dave Halliwell, to offer his services as manager.

It seemed like the start of something but, to Richard's frustration, Nick and Sobbo were rarely around. They weren't able to play another gig for almost a year. It's a tribute to his powers of persuasion that he was eventually able to make the rest of the band give up their 'sensible' career paths to come and join him on the dole in the hope that something might happen in the future.

Back in Wigan, without jobs or college, they were able to spend almost all their time practising in a dark room at Splash Studios. "It stunk; it was freezing," Simon Jones remembered later. "We tried taking heaters down there, but it never helped much." All they did was just plug in and play, night after night, week after week.

Eventually Verve began getting regular gigs at venues like The Citadel and then The Boardwalk in Manchester. At the time, the big band in Wigan were a folk-punk act called The Tansads that enjoyed a reasonable following. So it was a small coup for Verve to get a slot supporting them but Richard didn't see it like that. "We're gonna blow 'em off the stage! This town ain't big enough for the both of us," he said in an interview with the local paper.

In a kind of farcical, mini-version of the later Blur/Oasis rivalry, local newspaper *The Wigan Reporter* eagerly picked up on this, interviewing them under the headline 'Band War Breaks Out!'

The Tansads were understandably confused. "The lead singer rang me up," Richard said to *Planet Rock* later, "and said 'You're acting like some Svengali. What are you doing?' This was just a charity gig at the Wigan Pier! This guy couldn't believe it. I said 'I'm selling the tickets, man! I'm doing the Don King bit. I'm hyping it!'"

Not long afterwards, they recorded their own demo in the living room of Simon Jones' parents' house. It included five songs: 'Sun The Sea', 'Your Back', Slide Away', 'Move Me', and 'The Higher You Go'. They decorated the tape with a drawing of naked, nymph-like female figures apparently rising out of somebody's hand and, on the back, they typed a surprisingly brisk summary of the band: "Verve are a four-piece all-male band from the Wigan area. This demo was recorded on an eight-track home studio."

Anybody who was interested was advised to call Simon Jones. They sent it off to numerous labels and the first one to respond was Norwich's Backs Records. They later became a more conventional label but at the time they were acting more as a distributor. They were part of what was known as The Cartel, a syndicate of different companies that worked with London's Rough Trade to distribute independently released records throughout the country.

"During that whole period, demos were coming in from labels and from bands and we were always on the look-out for stuff," Backs label manager Derek Chapman told the author. "Verve just arrived as a demo, literally in the post. We were really impressed at the time. We were getting a lot of demos and a lot of them, obviously, weren't very good! It was good enough for us to take notice and contact the band but it was a period when we didn't really have our own label. Also Rough Trade Distribution and The Cartel was beginning to come apart slightly so we were in a state of flux.

We were much more in a situation, at that point, of suggesting to bands that, rather than signing to a record label, 'Why don't you do it yourself? Why don't you set up your own little record label and release it on that?'" Derek continues. "To which the usual response is: 'Yeah, yeah! How do we do that then?' So at that point we said 'Well, you need to record something that you're proud of and ready to release.' And I think they must have pleaded poverty so we said we'd send them a few quid if it would help them get some more recording done. If I remember correctly we sent them £60, which is presumably what they asked for, because it's a funny amount otherwise! Maybe that was enough to get them into a studio or something. And at that point Dave Boyd, who we knew because he was working at Rough Trade as a label manager, was saying have you heard anything good and we said 'Well, there's this new band Verve' and next thing we knew he'd gone up to see them or something!"

The Tansads had got wind of the fact that Verve were getting some interest from a label and they, too, then got in touch with Backs Records. "They phoned up or sent a note saying 'We hear you're going to sign Verve,'" says Derek, 'you should sign us, we're far better than them. They're rubbish!'"

Derek had no further dealings with Verve. "If they used that £60 to record any demos we never got them in any form!" he says, endearingly. "I don't think we've got any claim on them anyway! It was a slightly fluid relationship but obviously things moved quite quickly over that short period of time [for them]."

Shortly after hearing about Verve. Dave Boyd got a new job at
Virgin Records but the fledgling band had no idea that word of
their talent was spreading. Even negative responses from major labels
were eagerly received as a sign that at least it was getting through to
somebody and they weren't just throwing their demo into the void.
By this time Madchester was dead and the brief period when
London A&R men were signing up anybody with a bowl haircut,
baggy jeans and a Northern accent was very much over.

"It was almost like the tumbleweed was blowing in Manchester
again," Richard said to *Planet Rock*. "All the A&R people had moved
out. The thing was dead. The North, again, was feeling isolated."

However, although the only other interest they had – from major
label WEA – came to nothing, the tape did fall into the hands of
another young talent scout, Miles Leonard who would soon end up
working with Dave Boyd at Virgin.

"At the time I worked at Chrysalis Records," he told the author.
"I'd just started there at the lowest scout position, which meant
going through bin-liners of tapes and making tea. After phoning
around a few rehearsal studios I heard about Verve and called around
and managed to get hold of their demo tape and I loved it. I really
fell in love with the songs that were on it."

Miles Leonard is now the boss of Parlophone Records,
coincidentally The Verve's record label once again, but way back
then he was far too low in the pecking order for his opinion to
carry too much weight.

"I took them in to the head of A&R at the time who pretty much
dismissed it," he says. "I asked if I could go up to Wigan to see them,
even if it was just on a coach and back the same evening and it was
pretty much a resounding 'no'. It just so happened that I'd applied
for a job at Virgin at the same time and they phoned me up and said:
'Are you happy there?' and I said 'Funnily enough, not entirely.' So
they said 'Come and talk to us' and I said 'I've heard this band Verve
and I think they've got a really great demo and all I want to do is
go and see them and check them out.' Virgin and went up and saw
Verve at The Boardwalk in Manchester and thought they were just
incredible. Sonically they were like nobody else and Richard, even
though there was only a handful of people in the room, performed

as though he was in front of 75,000 in a stadium. It was almost as though he didn't care or couldn't see how many people were there."

Miles met the band and said they looked like "a mad bunch". Richard had a skinhead and wore a big bubble coat. He was worried that this London A&R man wouldn't know what to make of them but Miles didn't need any more convincing. He persuaded them that they should come down to London to play in front of the rest of Virgin's A&R team. The immediate problem was they could barely scrape together the money for petrol and Virgin weren't quite confident enough in their new recruit to forward the band any money for expenses. Miles was also worried that if they played in London, another A&R person might come in with a rival offer.

"I knew somebody who was booking shows at The King's Head on the corner of Fulham Palace Road," he says. "It was a venue that wasn't the obvious place for new up-and-coming bands to play at that point. That was The Falcon or the Bull & Gate or The Dublin Castle but I didn't want any other labels to see them either." Verve managed to make it down to the capital and play at The King's Head.

They were third on the bill to a jazz-funk band but seven or eight of the twenty people there were down from Virgin to see them. "Again, it was an incredible performance," remembers Miles. Also there was Dave Boyd who was so impressed he agreed to sign them straight away. In the early Nineties, signing to a major label, even a subsidiary like Hut, was still vaguely controversial in certain independent circles. For all their scruples about retaining artistic control, though, none of the band had any qualms about the move. Richard's attitude was always that as long as a band were good enough, the label would have to do what they wanted, rather than the other way round.

"You're still working for the man," he admitted years later in an interview with Darren Taylor of *Rock Sound*. "He might be smoking a spliff and his pony tail's in his back pocket but you're still working for him. But you've got to get in there. You shouldn't be afraid and feel like you've sold out. Often you're the thing that everyone buzzes on working with because they have to work with crap most of the day. They work with boy bands and they can use you as an excuse: 'Yeah, we might work with them but he's the man!'"

Virgin formed the Hut imprint largely so they could sign bands exactly like Verve. Their roster was made up of the relics of Madchester and various other bands that few people cared about. It was proving difficult to attract new talent. By giving it another name, they were also trying to make the point that they weren't just another major label preparing to squeeze every drop of life out of their bands. Although there's a lot of cynicism about these pseudo-indie labels, Verve were genuinely given a lot of independence and space.

Their second London gig was at The Falcon in Camden, the throbbing heart of everything vaguely indie; they were supporting one of the also-rans of the so-called 'shoe-gazing' scene, Whirlpool. 'Shoe-gazing' was the rather derogatory name given to the vogue for bands who, taking their cue from the likes of My Bloody Valentine, created a wash of guitar noise crested with blissed-out, hazy vocals. The main players were groups like Ride, Chapterhouse and Slowdive and, even though Verve had little in common with them, they were quickly lumped into the same scene.

NME journalist Roger Morton was there to review the headliners but it was Verve who would make a lasting impression. "It was revelatory," he told the author for this book. "It was one of those gigs where I had no expectations about anything. I was sent to do a live review of Whirlpool but the commissioning editor at the time said 'The support band are supposed to be of some interest so, if you're down there early enough and you want to write about them, go ahead.'

I got there early and there were about eight people in the room. I had no idea what to expect and then Verve came on and they were *astonishing*. Richard got off stage and he was in the middle of the floor — there was a lot of room because there was basically no audience! But it was a full-on gig with all their space-rock madness. He was just clearly a very singular, special frontman. In terms of charismatic frontmen from up north, the model was Ian Brown but his whole thing was completely different. He had a completely different presence from what Richard Ashcroft was doing — the cosmic, messianic, spaceman lunatic thing. It was really exciting to see somebody doing that. And they had this guitarist who was creating this whole cosmic rock world around it. I thought it was brilliant and I wrote a review which, I hope, said that!"

Verve played more London gigs, they had a great label behind them and soon enjoyed their first exposure in the national press – it seemed like things were happening exactly as they'd planned. On Valentine's Day 1992, they were booked to support Smashing Pumpkins on tour. It started well. Of all the bands who'd emerged out of the 'grunge' scene, the Pumpkins were probably the closest to Verve. In Billy Corgan they had a vocalist who also had a reputation for being slightly unpredictable and their sound had epic, almost prog-influences that took them a long way from the punk and metal roots of grunge. Richard was surprised to find that they ended up quite liking the Americans. He'd never particularly enjoyed meeting other bands. Often he just didn't feel he had much in common with them. But James Iha, the Smashing Pumpkins' guitarist, even presented Richard with a blouse with a butterfly motif as a token of his esteem.

Unfortunately, at the gig at London's Astoria they were told that they had to play at 7.30p.m, much earlier than planned, and there was no time for a soundcheck. As they swaggered on stage, most of their friends were still on their way down from Wigan. Their set ended up being cut short and a furious Richard smashed a bottle of vodka on stage before storming off bellowing, "They've turned us off but we've turned you on!"

In response, they immediately cancelled their planned tour with Catherine Wheel. They weren't prepared to deal with the acceptance of second best that is a normal part of being a support band. "Why should we put up with all that crap?" Richard demanded in another *Melody Maker* feature. "We're always telling people that we're a special band so why should people have to see us in those circumstances?"

Refreshingly, Richard admitted later that they weren't always the easiest people for the label to work with. "I was like a caveman," he said to *Planet Rock*. "Literally, loin cloth, no shoes, chunk of hash. Arrive in London [points]: 'I hate you', 'I hate you'. I'm not doing that. I'm not miming in videos. We were difficult people to work with."

Instead of touring, then, they went into Impact Studios in Canterbury to record their first single 'All In The Mind'. "We didn't want to go to a big name producer because we wanted to keep the edge and the rawness of what the band were about," says Miles Leonard. "So we decided to go for Paul Schroeder who'd engineered with John Leckie on the Stone Roses album. He really understood what the band were about and was very passionate and excited about them."

Despite this, the band, Nick in particular, found it frustrating that the sounds they managed to capture on tape didn't quite match the sounds they heard in their heads. It may not have helped that the sounds they heard in their heads were dramatically influenced by the LSD they'd been taking. "Verve recorded their first record on acid. That's not something that I would advise for most people going into the studio for the first time," Richard deadpanned many years later.

"It was at a time when there was a lot of experimentation, musically as well as recreationally," says Miles. "The two almost went hand in hand. That first session did have its ups and downs and there were outside influences [drugs] that came into that session and that had advantages and it had disadvantages too. It became quite a tense and odd recording session. There was a lot of pressure on the band. They'd just been signed to a major label and their ambition and drive at that point was greater than what they were capable of putting down on tape.

Even now if a band goes into the studio for the first time, it's very daunting. I think there's a lot of pressure to get things right. They were going through all those emotions and adding those highs and lows into that [mix] made things even more complicated. But the result was that 'All In The Mind' came out sounding as it should and 'Man Called Sun' ended up sounding even better. It was quite fast and energetic on the demo but it ended up being this quite tripped-out, stoned, ethereal sort of sound."

'All In The Mind' was unlike anything else out there. It had a rock 'n' roll swagger allied to a weird dreamlike quality. It didn't take things on quite the trip that some of their later singles would – it had a chorus, for a start, but it also had a guitar sound which stretched out in an eerie drone and a break-down which sounded like it belonged on a dance record.

The next track, 'One Way To Go' wasn't quite as good. The

bassline was more reminiscent of The Cure than anything else but with a slightly sleepy chorus repeated over the top by Richard.

But it was 'Man Called Sun' which would really divide people. It slows things down to Pink Floyd pace with Richard's spacily detached vocal drifting over Nick's chiming guitar. It was closer to ambient bands of the time like The Orb than it was to the popular indie bands like The Wonder Stuff. It was hippy music, basically – several minutes of blissed-out drifting. Richard's voice is gentle and weirdly insinuating and Nick's effects pedals are brilliantly employed to stop the guitar ever sounding remotely rock. The song appears to be going nowhere but, despite this, has its own ominous power which is reinforced by the ringing of a bell towards the end.

They were happy with the sessions, but Nick in particular always thought they could do better. In a radio interview with BBC London's Gary Crowley, Richard Ashcroft admitted that they were a little intimidated by the complexity of the recording studio.

"You walk in there and it's Cape Canaveral," he said. "You're just praying that the guy who seems to know what he's doing has a sense of where you're coming from."

Throughout their career, Verve recording sessions involved tremendous creative tension, which was only exacerbated by their narcotic intake. Their first visit to a studio would set the template for that.

"The pressures of that first recording started to show the personalities within the band," says Miles. "They were all finding their positions. For Richard this was an opportunity – the band were off. Nick always had an issue with trying to recognise and believe that what they were doing was great. He was always trying to make things better. It was almost as if he could hear something stronger or better in his head but he could not quite achieve it. Even from that first session Nick wouldn't go in and play something and think that was amazing and that was his job done. You started to see the early seeds then of real encouragement and push from the rest of the band, especially Richard."

At around the same time, Richard had a chance meeting with somebody else who would have a big impact on The Verve's career, sleeve designer Brian Cannon. "I first met him when he was 17," Brian told the author for this book, "and he was super cool. I was into all the football fashion of the time, I was a bit older than him and he was what I would describe as being like a *student*, with a flowery cap on his head. He went to college with a girl I was going out with and we met at a party in Wigan. He was fascinated by the fact that I designed record sleeves and that I set out to design record sleeves. I remember him saying to me 'Most fellas want to be footballers, DJs or rock 'n' roll stars and you actually went out to be a sleeve designer'.

He saw some of the work I did for (Manchester hip-hop outfit) Ruthless Rap Assassins and we had a chat and I thought nothing more of it. I didn't bump into him again for another two years. It was a remarkable coincidence, I was at a petrol station at six o'clock in the morning buying a pint of milk and I bumped into Richard Ashcroft and he's like: 'No fucking way! Brian Cannon! I spoke to you years ago. We've just been signed. Speak to our manager, David Halliwell, we want to work with you.' So that's how it all came about."

Brian started meeting up with Richard to discuss his ideas for their first sleeve together and he also met up with many of Verve's entourage, including Miles Leonard. Ultimately the designer decided to base the sleeve for 'All In The Mind' on a surreal, warped version of the strange life they were living at the time. It's a picture of the band and their friends sitting in what is essentially Richard's flat – except it's been removed and plonked in the middle of a park in Wigan. To make things more bizarre, they're all dressed up in surreal costumes and the picture is a strange, sinister colour.

"I came up with this bonkers idea of photographing all us lot in the park," Brian says. "It was January and it was fucking freezing and Miles Leonard was wearing a pair of Speedo shorts and nothing else except a pair of goggles and a fishing-gun. And it was cold! But we came out with the results. For the band's first single, that was a result. I just thought, *You need some kind of bizarre vision for this kind of music.* I worked with Oasis and Suede and Super Furry Animals in the Nineties and the music was always the inspiration. Otherwise you're cheating the band and the public."

Part of Richard Ashcroft's genius throughout his career has been his ability to inspire those around him to throw themselves into whatever they are doing. This was evident right from the start in the way that he managed to get friends to do the most ridiculous things for their sleeve shoots.

"Dave Halliwell was dressed up as a postman and I'm in a pair of shorts and a scuba outfit with a harpoon on top of one of the statues," remembers Miles. "They had Richard's flat laid out in the park including the floor tiles – that was everything that was in his flat."

"It's a great shot," photographer Michael Spencer Jones (who ended up doing almost all of The Verve's later sleeve photos) told the author for this book. "It's one of my favourite photographs. It's a really ambitious, Cecil B DeMille photo shoot. I shot it in colour first but it lacked atmosphere. You'd look at it and it just looked like a bunch of people dressed up in fancy dress in the park. But I shot some infra-red and that created this almost Hieronymus Bosch scene. It took it out of this world and into another world where it became more relevant."

The picture was highly appropriate. 'All In The Mind' represented a synthesis of everything Verve had been listening to and, perhaps, ingesting at the time. It was like turning their collective brains inside-out. The biggest influences were probably the Happy Mondays, the Stone Roses and My Bloody Valentine, as well as earlier bands who'd influenced them, such as Can. But they also had their own chemistry which people noticed even before they heard the music.

"When I first met them they had this energy to them like they were a unit," says Michael. "They were very young, eighteen or nineteen years old but they had a confidence that I'd not really seen before – it wasn't a cocky confidence, they just seemed very sure of themselves and they gelled very well as a band. To everybody around them at the time, it was clear that they were going to do something. There was no doubt that they were going to break through. There was an atmosphere around them."

Only a few years later, with the UK in the midst of Britpop fever, most new bands would take their influences from mainstream sources like The Beatles or the Kinks but in 1991, when Verve wrote 'All In The Mind', to be so obviously retro was pretty much unthinkable. Dance music was king and many rock bands were struggling to compete with it, either by providing blissed-out 'come down' music like the so-called shoe-gazing bands or by creating weird, psychedelic sounds.

Verve did both. There were elements of the rock that they also, secretly, loved – particularly in Sobbo and Simon Jones' powerful Led Zeppelin-influenced rhythm section; but their main aim was to soundtrack the highs and the come-downs of the kind of parties they used to have. Richard was often criticised for his lyrics, which perhaps made too much use of 'drug' metaphors about flying high in the sky but to be fair that, too, came straight out of dance music culture. Like the Stone Roses and the Happy Mondays, they wanted to express the spirit of rave culture through guitar, bass and drums.

This comes across particularly in the video for 'All In The Mind' which uses blurred visuals and rapid camera movements for a dance-y, psychedelic feel. Although Richard, waving his arms about dementedly, clearly wants to be a rock star, it's not at all clear that Verve want to be a 'rock' band in a traditional sense. They still weren't prepared to make even the tiniest compromises. When the director asked them to mime they tried but, somehow, it just didn't seem to work.

"We couldn't do it," Richard said to *Planet Rock*. "They had to bring gear in and we played a different song so in the 'All In The Mind' video, you see my mouth singing a different song because the concept of miming was making us feel incredibly uncomfortable, almost like we were selling out."

They were very far from selling out. They were, in fact, still doing exactly what they wanted. This might have limited their audience but their sound picked up a small but avid early following, even in the more Anglophile corners of America. Virgin set up a new American offshoot and that year Verve flew over to meet them at New York's annual CMJ music biz festival. To their glee, they were booked into the famous Chelsea Hotel where the likes of Jim Morrison used to hang-out and Sid Vicious allegedly killed Nancy Spungen.

The label hired them an open-top truck and they began jamming on a slow tour around central Manhattan. This was a time when the centre of Manhattan was still a dark, edgy place – before Zero Tolerance policing and tourist friendly crime figures. There were hookers and pimps dancing to the music pumping out of the wobbling speakers and shouting at them as they drove past.

"We thought 'God, we've just arrived!'" says Miles. "All of a sudden they're playing 'Man Called Sun' on a truck through Times Square. [Although] it wasn't this really expensive big truck that The Stones would have had. It was this ropey old thing with a cheap sound-system on it. Those were really exciting times!"

"I was out of my mind on the back of the truck, doing some insane jam, and thousands of people were just hanging around, getting into it," Richard said later. It was the moment that everybody around the frontman started to really share his belief that this might happen. "All of a sudden, it just seemed real," Dave Halliwell, their manager at that time, enthused. "You're in a band and you can actually do things. And someone is paying you."

Things seemed to be taking off. The week 'All In The Mind' was released, they made their first appearance on the front cover of a music magazine, *Melody Maker*. It was the start of a very odd relationship. There were few real stars at the time and certain writers eagerly leapt on the charisma and presence of Verve. Nevertheless, there were many others who viewed them with suspicion and even derision. This was partly because, in the space of one week, Richard told both main music papers that he thought one day he'd be able to fly.

"I believe you can fly and I believe in astral travel," he told Roger Morton of *NME*, "because, if I thought I was just going to walk around this place for the next 50 years, I don't think I could exist."

It was basically a statement of his belief that he could do whatever he set out to do. He'd learnt from his stepdad that it was important to believe nothing was impossible. Friends and staff at Hut later tried to clarify things on his behalf by claiming that he'd meant he could fly "through his music." But that's not quite it. He genuinely had a faith in the power of the mind, which, while it might have been absurd, also propelled him on to great things. In the short-term, though, it led to him being dubbed 'Mad Richard'.

"The *NME* grabbed at that whole thing of him believing literally that he could fly but it was just a passing comment," Roger explained to the author. "It was good for them, it helped people get the vibe of the whole thing. No harm done really. I don't know if he really literally thought he could fly! He was a good interview, not mad exactly, just a bit out there."

Despite this being good publicity, it did annoy Richard a bit. "I was known as 'Mad Richard' for four years in the British press," he said to Corey duBrowa of *Magnet* magazine much later. "Let's just make him a cartoon character, because that's where he's got to stay. We've got to box him off now and keep him there, because this kid's got too much of an imagination. And that's what they're scared of, that's what everyone's scared of. That's what neo-conservative rock is scared of, people with imagination that are gonna try to turn one person on, because that one guy might go on to change the fucking world, you know?"

CHAPTER 3

MAD RICHARD

Those who knew Richard Ashcroft in the early days are adamant that he wasn't 'mad' in any accepted sense of the term. No one was seriously implying this. His publicist at this time, Phill Savidge, says that the first word that comes to mind when he thinks of the Verve is "Northern". He believes that much of their intensity just came from a passionate love of music.

"A lot of London bands seem to be in it for reasons other than to do with the music," Phill explained to this author. "They could almost imagine their future on *Top Of The Pops* and on the cover of a music paper before they could imagine recording a fantastic song. Of all the bands I've met, Verve were more real than any of them and cared about the music more than anybody else. They had a drive for a sound they wanted to achieve."

Nevertheless Richard wasn't a typical musician, either. In the early days, the people who worked with him often remarked on the fact that he rarely had anywhere long-term to live or many possessions other than the clothes on his back.

"When he was living in Wigan, Brian Cannon must have lived about three miles from Richard Ashcroft," remembers photographer Michael Spencer Jones. "Brian's flat was an open house, everyone used to just turn up there, and one summer evening Richard walked from his flat to Brian's in his bare feet. Because he just liked walking around in bare feet. There are not many people who'd go on a three mile walk in the city like that. I remember Brian mentioning it to me like, 'He's not an ordinary guy!'"

Richard once even claimed that he travelled all the way down from Wigan to the record label in London without any shoes. "He [also] came into our office with no shoes on," says Phill. "I never thought it was that odd. You used to see a lot of strange sights then!

I did wonder if he'd come all the way down with no shoes or whether he'd just taken them off to come into the office. But he wasn't mad at all. Occasionally he'd come into the office with a hip-flask of whisky and he'd roll spliffs there quite a lot but he wasn't in the least bit 'mad'. I just think he was young and having fun."

His controversial quotes didn't bother the publicist either. "I thought it was absolutely fine," Phill says. "It wasn't doing any harm. A few years later, when we looked after Kula Shaker, [vocalist] Crispian Mills ruined his career by saying that he liked the swastika as an Indian peace symbol. By saying those words he destroyed his career. Richard never said anything like that."

Unlike Crispian, who genuinely outraged people with his ill-advised comments, all Richard faced was ridicule. *Melody Maker* once wrote a comic article entitled 'The Crazy World Of Richard Ashcroft' in which they printed a slightly odd list of five things that indicated he was a bit of a loony. These were: refusing to wear underpants, sleeping on Simon's floor, being thrown out of music class for playing the glockenspiel with chopsticks and helping out in a hairdressers where some clients supposedly suspected he was gay.

The music Verve created on their first EPs and singles, not to mention the videos they produced for them, fitted with the description of them by Noel Gallagher as "a bunch of space cadets led by Captain Rock."

For their second single, 'She's A Superstar', they moved up to a more expensive studio, The Manor near Oxford. "That was a really amazing session," says Miles. "There was lots of experimentation recreationally and within the music. Listen to the B-side of 'She's A Superstar' – 'Feel' – they recorded that in an indoor swimming pool and when the sounds go all echoey, it was because they were recording in there at the time. They always wanted to push the boundaries."

They also inspired Brian Cannon to push the boundaries with the sleeve design. The artwork for 'She's A Superstar' might well be the best image on any of their sleeves. They liked it so much that they later used a similar image for the cover of the *This Is Music* singles collection. It features what looks like a powerful waterfall streaming down a hillside in a blur before splashing over a neon 'Verve' sign. Meanwhile, the four members of Verve are barely visible as dots on the horizon.

"That was a particular favourite of mine," says Brian. "That's a remarkable sleeve even though I do blow my own trumpet. We came up with the idea of this cascading waterfall and we drove all the way to the Pennines in south Derbyshire to find the right location. You've got to bear in mind at this point that none of it was done in [image manipulation software] Photoshop. It was all real. That was one thing we prided ourselves on. We never did anything digitally. I had this neon sign made in Manchester and we transported it to the Derbyshire hills. It looks like that waterfall's about 30 feet high. It's actually about six feet high. And you see how blue the water is? I was stood upstream with a dustbin full of blue food colouring which I poured into the river and that's what gave it the blue effect. And that's the band actually stood in the background. There's no digital enhancement going on whatsoever. We shot it for real. It took us days to work out. It took us days to find the location."

"When I shot the 'All In The Mind' sleeve, it was the coldest shoot ever," says Michael Spencer Jones. "It was absolutely freezing. My hands were so cold that I could hardly operate the camera and it took three or four hours to shoot. That set a precedent for really cold photo shoots. So when we came to do 'She's A Superstar', it was the same. It was March in the middle of the moors in Derbyshire and I got them to stand on top of a hill right in the background and they just stood there while I was pottering around with the waterfall. Eventually they came down but none of them had mobile phones so we were communicating by sign language. They were so cold that Richard said he felt like a piece of earth!"

Despite all the effort they'd put into the music and corresponding artwork, the nine minutes of 'She's A Superstar' confused a lot of people. Nick's melancholic slide guitar suddenly brought in new country influences but they were far more distorted and otherworldly than any 'normal' country record. As the song goes on, it keeps sounding like it's about to explode with long wails of feedback and moments with a much rockier sound. Then it dives downwards again as Richard emotes dreamily over the top.

Like many of their early songs, tracks like 'She's A Superstar' and 'Man Called Sun' would never sound the same way twice when played live, so the version they captured on record was just a snapshot. There's a sense on the early singles that the whole band are deferring musically to Nick, letting him dictate their sound with his carefully controlled blasts of guitar feedback or delicately plucked chords. Richard's lyrics were deliberately vague and trippy because, rather than using them to talk about his own life – as he would later – he was trying to find words that fitted with the band's music. This led to a certain amount of criticism because, perhaps, it was easier to capture the altered mental state they were aiming for with a guitar than with words.

Interestingly when they played 'She's A Superstar' live later on, Richard's vocal would be much higher in the mix and with the slide guitar it's then much easier to see the similarities with 'The Drugs Don't Work'. It even suggests what 'The Drugs Don't Work' might have sounded like if Nick McCabe had been more involved. The main difference is that these early records gave Nick the opportunity to go wherever he wanted live, without having to feel like he needed to stick to a rigid structure.

Just a couple of songs into their career and Verve already seemed to be finding a niche as a cult band. They would always have a devoted following but they were initially a little too weird for the mainstream. Even their own audience must have found them a frustrating band at times. In 1993 they supported kindred spirits Spiritualized and Richard was blown away by frontman Jason Pierce's own blissed-out voyaging. Just a few years before, Pierce had broken up his highly influential first band Spacemen 3 and Spiritualized's 1992 debut album *Lazer Guided Melodies* had been equally acclaimed.

Spacemen 3 had once recorded a demo tape called *Taking Drugs To Make Music To Take Drugs To*, which gives some indication of their agenda. They'd certainly been influential on the whole shoe-gazing scene. Their minimalist take on rock music, reducing it to a few droning chords and a deliberately anti-star aesthetic, was as significant as My Bloody Valentine's expanded use of feedback. Although they never broke through into the mainstream, their sound and style had inspired dozens of bands circa 1993.

On *Lazer Guided Melodies*, Jason Pierce's new band, including his new girlfriend Kate Radley on keyboards, took country and gospel as a starting point and distilled them to their essence, repeating simple variations in sound like a mantra, blasting them out in a massive wall of sound. This was the kind of thing Richard wanted Verve to be doing. It was rock as a conduit to the kind of higher state of consciousness that, in the Nineties, was mostly the province of dance music.

Maybe he suddenly felt the pressure but, at one support slot in Norwich, Verve only played two songs before leaving the stage explaining that "it just wasn't happening." Richard was confident that crowds would share his belief that a gig had to be all or nothing but inevitably there were dissenters. "We played in Norwich," he told *Melody Maker*, "and this guy comes up and says, 'Can I tell you something?' so I said, 'Yeah, all right,' and he said, 'I think you're a cock.' And I thought, 'Wow! I'd moved this guy.' I'd much rather that than, 'I thought the gig was all right.'"

Derek Chapman, the Backs label manager who'd sent the band 'a few quid', also saw them for the first time then and was astonished. "Richard was in a bit of a mood that night," he says, "and I think they only did about two numbers but it was magnificent. I remember thinking 'That's the best two-song set I've ever seen a band do.' They were really on fire. Then they stormed off stage for some reason and I can't remember why. Nick's guitar was incredible. I thought 'That's a sound I haven't heard since Jimmy Page.' Richard was doing a lot of leaping up and down and then they stormed off. It was a great finale."

Verve were dividing opinions wherever they went. Another gig later on during the tour at the Town & Country Club in London saw most of the set taken up with a 25 minute jam. Richard had become friends with Jason and Kate but he was also deeply competitive. "He wanted to out-Spiritualize Spiritualized," says Phill Savidge.

Most of the other representatives from the music industry were just bemused. Nobody could work out whether Verve were brilliant or completely ridiculous. This band had a frontman who clearly wanted to be a huge star but the music they were making was so far from being radio-friendly that it was hard to see how that would be possible.

As *Melody Maker* wrote at the time: "Do McCabe and Co. possess sufficient technical savvy to contrive the kind of zippy, snappy pop they're going to need to reach a larger audience and give Ashcroft the adoring following he deserves? Or are Verve doomed to languish on the margins, three musicians with credibility plus one exhibitionist without a public? We'll see."

Considering what would happen in the future, it was a very astute observation but, at the time, Dave Boyd, the boss of their label Hut, was worried about them. Six months after being signed, he thought that they needed guidance. Richard claimed later that he had "the most ridiculously indulgent, decadent six months." In reality this just meant that he ate takeaway lasagne every day (because you get bored of pizza, apparently). This was not a band of extravagant tastes.

"I didn't see them living the high life," says Miles. "That thing with Richard wearing no shoes was pretty much because he had no shoes! If you went up to Richard's [home] in Wigan, it was a tiny little flat above a chemist. It was a cool flat but it wasn't anything ostentatious, far from it, it was second-hand furniture and old carpets and mattresses on the floor. That was how they lived. It was either that or they lived with their folks still. They drove around in a battered old van. It was always breaking down. I think they were relieved when they went into a studio or on tour because it meant that they had a hotel or a studio to stay in. They knew they were going to have somewhere to live and something to eat."

That would be the case for the next few years. Even on the cover of [the much later] single, 'This Is Music', you can see that Richard wasn't spending a lot of money on new clothes. "I love the fact that if you look at the cuffs on the guy's jacket, they're frayed," says Brian Cannon. "That was no student thing. He was fucking skint basically. He had no money to buy a new jacket."

Verve were still very young and had little idea about accounting or the business side of the music industry. Dave Boyd decided to ask John Best, then a successful publicist with PR firm Savage and Best, if he'd be interested in the managerial reigns of Verve.

John Best told the author in an interview for this book that, "They'd spunked [most of] their money, only about six months after they'd signed. It wasn't a lot of money [but] they just split the money four ways and went off and spent it and then went 'What do we do now?' Dave Boyd asked me if I'd be their manager and I was sceptical because I'd never been a manager."

John and business partner Phill went to see them at one of their early London gigs and they were blown away. "There weren't many people there and Richard was crouching on the floor for most of it," Phill remembers. "He was a combination of confident and shy – the same way Michael Stipe used to perform with his hands behind his back as though he was thinking, *I'm doing this under duress.* Richard had a way of doing it as well, which was curling into a shell on stage. He still does the same thing fifteen years later to 50,000 people. Then it was just twenty people and I remember it being really, really impressive."

"Occasionally a band would turn up, like Suede, and just from the moment you saw them you knew it was going to work," says John. "With Verve, I thought, *This is definitely going to work!* It was Richard's self-belief and sense of self. Music had been very anti-star for a long time. There was a post-punk hangover where a rock star was seen as a flamboyant arsehole into cocaine and money and all that kind of stuff. That really lasted all the way through the Eighties with bands like My Bloody Valentine and shoe-gazing bands where there was no star quality whatsoever. That was what was cool. Then suddenly Brett Anderson came along and I thought, *Holy shit!* I hadn't seen a frontman for ages. Then all of a sudden you'd got Jarvis Cocker and Richard Ashcroft."

Many critics hated Verve for exactly the same reason. In a 1992 live review, *Melody Maker*'s Everett True scoffed "I thought the whole idea of wanting to be a rock star was discredited. Obviously not."

Although the idea of the star was suddenly very much in vogue, few frontmen could actually pull it off. Whether they liked him or not, virtually all critics were forced to admit that Richard's performance was unlike anything else they'd seen. "[He] shimmies down the line between shaman and shitehawk more precariously than any of the other new indie narcissists," observed John Mulvey in *NME*.

"It's not feasible that he can have taken as many drugs as his performance, a mixture between Bobby Gillespie and severe mental handicap, suggests," quipped Stuart Maconie in the same magazine.

Verve were in the enviable position that even their unfavourable reviews made them sound interesting and there were plenty of rave reviews, too. Michael Spencer Jones remembers those early gigs as being quite incredible.

"They were a great band to be around," he says. "The gigs they were doing '92, '93 and '94 were absolutely amazing. Just *amazing*. I always felt that they never captured that on the records. Some of those gigs they did reached points where it was elevated to a completely different place. Nick would come out with this amazing guitar work which would fire up Richard and they'd be taking off, going in a direction which you'd never heard them go before. Halfway through a gig they'd break all this new musical ground and blow audiences away. At the end of the gig you'd go 'What was that?' No two gigs that they did were ever the same. They'd always go off on a tangent."

Savage and Best (sic) eventually agreed to take over Verve's management and PR but things still didn't happen as fast as hoped. Suede's debut single 'The Drowners' had comprehensively eclipsed them in the minds of the music press and made the old shoe-gazing scene – which Verve were still erroneously associated with – seem painfully out-dated.

"We were looking after a lot of the shoe-gazing stuff, which was Moose and Lush and Curve," says Phill. "Verve emerged from that but they always hated being lumped together, as did everybody. Richard was much more of a showman than the rest of them. The only thing that was shoe-gazey about them was a meandering sound that could go on and on. A song could go on for ten minutes. But generally the shoegazing bands had singers who played guitar – they weren't looking at their shoes, they were looking at their chords. Richard didn't do that so he couldn't be a typical shoegazing singer." The second single eventually reached number 66 in the charts, a start of sorts.

The band's third single, 'Gravity Grave', wasn't ten minutes but it still had that trippy, mellow style only with a more sinister edge to it. It starts with a bass-line that could belong in a Led Zeppelin song, pure rock 'n' roll, then Richard's voice and McCabe's guitar compete with each other to see who can sound the most psychedelic, spaced-out and dreamlike, over the top.

In their early writing process, Verve would jam, sometimes for up to an hour, and then it would be Richard's job to arrange the best moments that they'd come up with into something like a structure. On 'Gravity Grave', it's not so much a song as a snapshot of the band playing.

Nevertheless, Verve's early singles were far more than just practice sessions on the way to later glories. There's a balance to the early tunes, with each member of the band contributing, that they perhaps lost later. Listening to the live versions, particularly, it's not hard to see why Nick McCabe felt musically constricted by their more structured recordings. One thing that let them down for many critics was the lyrics, but at this point Richard was just trying to come up with imagery that fitted the music. With its lyric about the setting sun, 'Gravity Grave' is another reminder of the parties the band and their friends used to have on the beach. This image is reinforced by Brian Cannon's cover art – a picture of a beach with a trail of clothes leading up to a naked man, in the distance, about to walk into the water. In the foreground, slightly sinisterly, there's a clock embedded in the sand and the word 'Verve' carved out of wood.

"We shot 'Gravity Grave' on Formby Beach in Lancashire," Brian says. "It's an astonishing place. If you look at the sleeve, it looks like the Bahamas or something. There's this guy called B who was our friend and the Verve's friend and we paid him a bottle of vodka to get involved. He drank it and stripped off – thus the naked man on the beach. It all looks quite surreal. There's a guy with no fucking clothes on, pissed out of his head walking towards the sea, while we'd crafted together the wooden letters in the sand. People always said to me 'it's so Dali-esque' but only because there's a clock involved. I love Salvador Dali. I love him to bits but it's got nothing to do with Dali, that sleeve."

"This time not only was it freezing but we got the main person to take his clothes off!" remembers Michael Spencer Jones. "He was going in the sea as well. The amount of good-will shown by people was amazing. That was a Reginald Perrin thing where this guy decided to leave everything behind and walk off into the ocean."

In the early Nineties, most bands who played 'indie' music secretly accepted that it would never have massive commercial appeal and so there was a spirit of adventure and experimentation.

Britpop still hadn't arrived to shift things back towards a more 'classic' traditional sound. Nevertheless, Richard felt that even in the small world of the indie scene, Verve weren't getting the attention they deserved.

"He'd come into the office and see on our wall [that] we'd have 200 front covers of everyone from Curve to Pulp to Suede and probably Elastica at that time as well," says their PR man Phill, "and I'm sure he must have thought *Why have we only got three covers when Suede have got eighteen before their first record comes out?* He must have thought that. Jarvis [Cocker of Pulp] and Brett [Anderson of Suede] were much easier to understand if you're a music journalist – who seem to be obsessed with lyrics rather than guitar chords. Verve were obsessed with guitar chords and the sound of words rather than what they mean."

In some early interviews, there are suggestions that the band felt Hut wanted to push them towards a more commercial sound but Miles Leonard says that this wasn't actually the case. "The songs they had were exciting and individual and unique and I didn't think anybody sounded like them," he says. "There wasn't a discussion to try and form that into a pop sound. I don't think that would have worked. What we needed was for the band to develop before we went to record an album. They needed to develop themselves and see what new songs would come through. It was really about making sure we could capture them sonically as best as we could against what they sounded like live. They were just this amazingly exciting live band who had these moments with these spaced-out riffs and we needed to make sure that was retained because that's what they were about."

"After the first single they [Hut Records] thought the next single was going to go flying into the top forty," Richard said to *Rock Sound* editor Darren Taylor, "and Dave [Boyd] comes down and hears an eight minute tune and, like, [sighs] he knows it's not going to get played on the radio! But it's a long-term thing."

Late in 1992, Verve played some of their biggest gigs so far, supporting retro rock band The Black Crowes at Brixton Academy. It was another strange pairing but then there weren't any other acts quite like Verve. There were some similarities. Both bands had certain hippyish qualities and a love of the Rolling Stones and early rock. Evidently something about the band impressed Richard. He aped Black Crowes' vocalist Chris Robinson's habit of playing barefoot on-stage. At the same time, he also developed the habit of ceremonially removing his jacket and shoes before he began to play.

"I don't like to think too much about it," Richard said to the *NME*, "otherwise it would all become too self-conscious. But I guess it's like a shedding of the skin, y'know? You take off your skin, abandon yourself, enjoy it, share this experience, and then you put the skin back on again and you're off."

Richard was still making grandiose claims in the press about being the biggest band in the world and playing to 40,000 people. With that in mind, when they came to record their album, they called on acclaimed producer John Leckie, who'd previously recorded the Stone Roses' seismic debut.

John Leckie started his career as an in-house engineer at Abbey Road, working with Pink Floyd and the solo projects of The Beatles, among many others. In the Seventies he became a producer and worked with post-punk bands like Magazine and XTC. He was known for his ability to get the best out of young bands but Verve would be a massive challenge. He'd seen them play at the Camden Falcon gig and he was well aware that it wouldn't be easy to capture their unique live sound on record.

"I just knew they were special," he said to Q magazine. "For days after, I kept thinking about this band and checking the music list to see when they wcrc playing again. They're the only band I've ever approached to work with. What really impressed me was the dynamics, how devastatingly loud they could be, and how quiet and sensitive they could be. At points you could hear a pin drop – and then it would just explode."

Verve were deeply unprepared for their debut album, with only three new songs written. Nevertheless they headed to Sawmills Studio in Cornwall and tried to make a record.

CHAPTER 4

STORMING HEAVEN

It was winter when Verve arrived at Sawmills, an old mill by the River Fowey in the middle of Cornwall. There was snow on the ground and the only way to reach the studio was by boat or, when the tide was out, by walking down the railway track. All of their gear had to arrive on that same boat and, if they weren't there on time, they'd have to wait another twelve hours for the tide to come in before they could bring it over. With the river on one side and thick woods on the other, Sawmills offered the isolation and lack of distraction that the band needed. As soon as they arrived, they had a feeling of being completely cut off from the world. It was inspiring but also slightly unnerving.

They began writing songs the only way they knew how, by jamming together, sometimes for hours, before Richard would lay down vocals over the top. John Best has a theory as to why Verve's early records sound so different to later, more straightforward tunes like 'History' and 'The Drugs Don't Work': "What happened was they'd jam and they'd have no lead vocal melody in the song and so you'd get this long instrumental work-out which Richard, when he came to rehearsal, would just scat over. And he had a good ability to just sing freeform over whatever's going on. He had that mantric quality. They're very good at that. They got a lot of buzz early on but then there was a theory put around by people like [music journalist] John Harris – 'They're a good band but why don't they ever write any songs?'"

With only three fresh songs written, the rest of the album had to come out of the extended jam sessions. In a way, Verve had too much integrity for their own good. They refused to put any of their earlier singles on the album, arguing that their fans had already paid for them once. The only problem with this stance was the fact that they then had to write virtually the entire album from scratch.

"We fucking deserve a medal," Simon Jones told *Exclaim!*, "because it was the hardest thing I've ever done in me life, to go and do a record when you have three songs." John Leckie might have deserved a medal, too, for dealing with the strong-willed band. Often when the producer would adjust Nick's amp, the guitarist would wait until he'd left the room before turning it back.

"I didn't notice tensions between John and the band at the time but that could have been Nick coming out of the studio and not being 100% happy with what they were trying to capture," says Miles Leonard. "He always wanted better. He always strove for more and he always felt it could be better. That's pretty much how I remember Nick. He wasn't always satisfied with the result, whether it was a recording or a live show. He always felt it could be much better.

I think they thought things were going well in the studio. I think John Leckie understood what they were trying to achieve and he was immensely passionate about the band. I think he captured the band as they were at that point. I only went back to that album recently and I realised how brilliant it is as a debut. The recordings were fantastic."

One suggestion to come from John Leckie was the addition of a horn section on several tracks. In the past he'd used celebrated session musicians The Kick Horns, who'd been working since the early Eighties. They were used to dealing with rock bands and weren't fazed by Verve's unorthodox working methods. One evening, about 10p.m. they walked along the railway track and arrived at the studio just as the band and John Leckie were listening to what they'd recorded so far in the tiny control room.

"My main memory is Richard Ashcroft," saxophonist Tim Sanders told the author. "He looks extraordinary because he's such a thin guy. Usually when we'd arrive for a session we'd aim to have a meeting, at least, or listen to some stuff in advance but as I remember we came in cold. I think what we were expecting was to have a listen to a few things that evening and then start work the next morning. What happened was we got going straight away and recorded late into the night and then had a few hours sleep and then did a bit more the next morning or the next afternoon!"

The atmosphere at Sawmills gave the recording sessions its own intense vibe. "It's the most magical place," flautist Simon Clarke told the author. "You walk down the railway line and then through the woods and down to this house which used to be a mill. It's got no roads to it and it's surrounded by trees and it overlooks a little mini-estuary, coming out from the main estuary, where the boat moors up. I can't remember whether we did it with [Verve] but sometimes people record outside. It's an amazing place to work because you really feel like you're cut off from the rest of the world. You can just disappear into your own thing."

Apart from one night when Richard and Sobbo managed to borrow a canoe and disappear down the river with a bottle of whisky, they threw themselves wholeheartedly into recording. The time there passed in a blur of music and hash.

"When it was all going on, I was in a corner of the room, looking down and sort of laughing at myself," Richard told *Cake* magazine. "It's such a surreal setting you can't help but get a kick out of being involved with it. It's like being involved in this ridiculous movie."

The band had never worked with other musicians before and they were excited to be able to add something new to the mix, taking the record away from basic rock. All of them loved a wide range of music and they didn't want to be trapped in one particular style. Despite the fact that the Kick Horns had only just got there, they did indeed start work straight away.

"I was very tired," says Tim, "and I would have preferred to have a little bit of time to think about stuff and maybe work fresh the next day, but in practise I think we got the best out of it by working there and then as the band wanted. They were pretty good at giving us a sense of what they were looking for. It was easy for us to interpret that. They were looking for texture and colour really more than melodic input. It was just the sound of the horns they wanted, really. Big slabs of stuff! They knew that we knew what we were doing and there was a level of mutual trust. They recognised we'd do our best for them. They were just excited about having some different sounds that they couldn't do themselves. What impressed me was that when they weren't working, they were always listening to music. I remember the next day at breakfast, there was a lot of music being played, a wide variety of stuff. They were a band who were open, who had open ears."

"They were totally into the music which is always so exciting," agrees Simon Clarke. "It's fantastic working with young bands when they're just so excited by it all. Leckie's a brilliant producer for that because he'll let bands run with it. He's somebody who's got great ears, who's got good ideas but he's also very good at letting people have their head and do their thing and let things go to interesting places."

For Verve, there sometimes wasn't much distinction between making music and rehearsing. Their jam sessions would often veer off into new territory and all of a sudden they'd find they'd got a new song. Because of that, the task facing them at Sawmills wasn't as onerous as it might have been.

"It was always a joy to hear Verve," says John Best. "You'd be in the rehearsal room and they'd come in from lunch or something and pick up their instruments and jam and out of it you'd watch a song being born. That was how they used to write."

"I remember it being a really enjoyable and positive experience," says Simon. "They sang some ideas at us and we came up with some ideas and John might have had some ideas and we adapted things as we went. It's kind of a mutual process, really."

Right the way through their career, one of the band's strengths – and particularly Richard's – was the ability to inspire and enthuse the people around him. The Kick Horns have worked with dozens of stars but Simon Clarke still remembers his first sessions with Verve as something special. "I remember it being a very intense experience," he says. "I remember going to the studio, working really hard but having a great time and feeling very uplifted and tired after a couple of days of doing music and thinking *That's amazing.*"

For all the band's occasional doubts, something exceptional came out of the concentrated, intense period of recording that produced the debut album – to be called *A Storm In Heaven*. Because all the songs were written and recorded in a short space of time, it had a coherence that, for all the brilliance of their later albums, they would never achieve again. Every member of the band knew what a Verve song sounded like and they were all pulling in the same direction.

The first track 'Star Sail' shows their total confidence in what they were doing. It doesn't try and beat the listener over the head. There's a deceptive blast of feedback and then a series of wordless cries from Richard against a slow, shimmering wave of guitar. When his vocal arrives, it's distant and confused, as though he's on the verge of losing his mind, stumbling blindly through the cosmos.

While there were lots of bands producing this kind of slow-burning spacerock in the early Nineties, not many had the underlying edginess that came out of this apparent confusion and spontaneity. There was something slightly safe about southern contemporaries like Ride and Slowdive but there was an unsettling, almost disturbed quality about Verve. This was probably what later inspired Hollywood producers to come calling. Bizarrely 'Star Sail' was later included in the much-derided Sharon Stone vehicle *Sliver*.

They also had a love of rock 'n' roll which came out in the second track 'Slide Away', a much more aggressive take on the same formula. Starting by sounding a bit like Ride, it's more dynamic and uneven. Nick exercises many of his different playing styles, from aggressive Led Zeppelin riffing to a completely blissed-out wall of sound.

The next track 'Already There' concentrates on the latter, building remorselessly upwards from feathery guitar into something that churns and grinds furiously before dropping back down again. Here, as on much of the album, it's not hard to tell that the vocals have been improvised on the spot. It almost sounds like beat poetry as Richard virtually speaks his lyric over the surface of the music, never reaching any kind of climatic chorus, fading out along with the music.

Then, with 'Beautiful Mind', there's a subtle change of direction towards something a bit more 'countrified'. The vocals are right at the back of the mix as Nick's slide guitar dominates, creating a feeling of woozy melancholia. It's not hard to imagine it gently lulling you into sleep but the intro of album highlight 'The Sun, The Sea' puts paid to that. It begins with a harsh guitar riff and, unexpectedly, a blast of horns. From then on Richard's most powerful vocal yet rides out over a Spaghetti Western landscape of ominous riffs and further blasts from the wind instruments. "Bringing in the horn section gives it almost that Miles Davis sound," Miles Leonard says. "That was something that John was brilliant at bringing to the party."

Anybody who wanted to make the point that Verve never wrote 'songs' would have a lot of ammunition with 'The Sun, The Sea'. Once again they don't reach any kind of chorus but do they need to? The song finishes with an exhilarating, discordant attack from the horn section and then a confused jangle of guitars.

The next track, 'Virtual World', goes even further out there. The basic rhythm treads water slightly but its overlaid, bizarrely, with a prog-rock style flute solo.

"I remember we had to be somewhere and we were a bit tight for time," says Simon Clarke, "so my memory of doing the flute on 'Virtual World' was that was the last thing we did. 'Oh, we've got to go in half an hour' ... 'Can you just try and play on this?' So I had a couple of passes at it and that was it, basically. Everybody was happy."

By 'Make It Till Monday', they'd gone as far into the dreamy ether as they possibly could. There's a bare shimmer of guitar in the background, some gentle riffs in front of that and then Richard's voice sounding like it's coming from a long way beyond the grave; weirdly serene and out there, tripping in opposite directions to the music.

'Blue', in contrast, is the closest thing they get to a pointer towards the next album. Its aggression and machismo had more in common with the tracks on *A Northern Soul* than anything else on *A Storm In Heaven*.

'Butterfly', too, threatens to rock with a raw, bluesy rhythm and powerful slide guitar before veering off into more psychedelic soundscapes as Richard is multi-tracked chanting the title. The name 'Butterfly', incidentally, went back to Richard's interest in chaos theory and the famous idea that a butterfly flapping its wings in one part of the globe could cause a tornado to appear in another. One of his first bands was called the Butterfly Effect and he was fascinated with the apparent scientific 'proof' of the interconnectedness of all things.

A Storm In Heaven's final track 'See You In The Next One (Have A Good Time)' was significant because it was the first track based around a song that Richard wrote on his own (on the sleeve notes, it is credited to The Verve). Unsurprisingly, it was quite different to everything else on the album, with a much cleaner sound. The vocals are still deliberately hazy and a long way back in the mix but the relative simplicity of the song prefigured what he would do later. Over a gentle piano melody, played by Nick, he croons gently, proving, as he'd always said, that the country rock of his solo albums didn't come out of nowhere.

When they recorded *A Storm In Heaven*, Nick was the oldest member of Verve at just 21. For such a young band it was an incredible achievement. Some groups take years to find their own distinct sound, many never do at all but Verve had managed it first time. Their perfectionism meant that they could never be entirely happy with the record. They would always wonder what they might have come up with if they'd had more time or if they'd been a bit less stoned. But, sometimes, pressurised environments produce the best results.

There were harsh suggestions that the resulting album was a compromise that nobody was entirely happy with but that might have just been a response to its eventual relatively poor sales or, perhaps, just the fact that it didn't reach the heights of their best gigs. "We were searching for things, and waiting for it to rain down on us," John Leckie would later say to *Select*. "We came close but neither they nor I thought they managed it. It lacked the overwhelming effect of the Verve experience, maybe as there was no audience to feed off."

But *A Storm In Heaven* is still far more than a trial run for later glories. Indeed, there are many people who regard it as the 'real Verve', before they 'went commercial'. When the first UK single off the album came out, the brilliant 'Blue', it destroyed the idea that they were a wishy-washy shoe-gazing band. It decisively left behind any comparisons with ambient music for a much heavier, louder sound. It was Richard's best vocal performance so far, perhaps because he appeared to have put so much thought into the lyrics. Nick's guitar, too, is suddenly aggressive and truculent. There are still elements of the dreaminess and trippiness of their earlier singles but 'Blue' is more like a bad trip or a nightmare. At times it sounds like Richard's offering a warning before, on their most powerful chorus so far, it turns into a taunt. What makes 'Blue' so great is that although it's clearly cut from the same stream-of-consciousness cloth as their other singles, it also has a sharp chorus with Richard exercising a falsetto that demonstrated his new confidence.

The video captures the vibe perfectly. Beginning with the band walking down into a party that appears to be held in some kind of cellar, it features an eerie little girl who looks like she belongs in *The Exorcist*. She's staring at them as Richard starts losing it spectacularly. In the end, as they walk out of the house and up into the cave featured on the cover of *A Storm In Heaven*, it's hard to tell whether they're as out of it as they seem or whether they're just acting.

It was John Best who came up with a highly appropriate title for their debut album after a book he was reading. "I had this conversation with Richard about what they were going to call the first album," he says, "and I had this book by Jay Stevens about LSD and how it was a shortcut to Nirvana and it was called *Storming Heaven* so I said you should call it 'storming heaven' because that's what your music does. I thought this was a good euphemism for what their music did and he changed it to *A Storm In Heaven*.

At one point, Hut boss Dave Boyd had wanted to save the image they used for the cover of 'She's A Superstar' for their debut album – he was so impressed by it. However, Brian Cannon and Michael Spencer Jones promised that they could come up with something even better. Spurred on by the magnificently overblown, psychedelic music, Brian Cannon resolved to come up with images and a concept to match. Along with Spencer Jones, he put almost as much effort into the sleeve as the band had into the music. On the front was a picture of a ghostly figure at the mouth of a cave in front of the letters VERVE in flames and then inside was a whole series of different vignettes of the band and their friends.

For the cover shoot they headed to Thor's Cave in Staffordshire. With its massive entrance, ten metres high and seven and a half metres wide the cave was a striking landmark at the top of a hill. The cave had an odd history. It was the site of several Palaeolithic graves and, according to legend, 8th century martyr St Bertram left his pregnant wife to take shelter there when she went into labour but, when he returned with a midwife, he found she'd been eaten by wolves. This kind of mythology appealed to the band but, more importantly, the cave looked amazing.

"I've done some serious covers for some serious bands but that's the best piece of work that I'll ever do," Brian Cannon says. "We worked double hard and I mean double hard on that. I used to go to Manchester when I was thirteen to buy records and if it had a gatefold sleeve you'd think, *Wow, this band's made the effort!* So I thought *We'll do a gatefold album sleeve.* We spent three or four months doing it and the whole point is it's the journey of life. On the cover – birth – the cave's like a vaginal opening in the mountain in the background. Then the next picture – the recklessness of youth – the band sitting there playing chess while there's a car on fire in the background. Then – the hopelessness of middle-life – with the guy sitting there watching TV. Then at the end – death with the guy in the graveyard. That's the journey of life. We spent months on that. We had no budget whatsoever! I think I got paid two grand for doing that!"

On all the sleeves so far the name of the band had been in the photograph somewhere rather than just written on afterwards. This time Michael Spencer Jones got a welder friend to make large metal letters which they lugged all the way up the hill.

"I'd always wanted to shoot a band in a cave," says Michael. "I thought it would make a great backdrop and I went for a walk with my girlfriend and came across this amazing place that I thought was such a great location for a band shoot. Then I realised that the best viewpoint wasn't looking into the cave, it was from inside looking out. By that point we'd established that we'd always have Verve incorporated in the photograph in the same way that Pink Floyd did and Brian came up with the idea of having letters on fire.

You've also got the contrast of the blue cave and the orange of the fire so it works on a colour level. By the time we'd done it, it was obvious that it looked like a womb so we thought we'd get a figure shining through at the end (a ghostly shape you can see in the background). It was a good way of introducing a human element without having somebody in the cave. When we'd done that, that got us on to the whole notion of the cycle of life thing. The concept came later!"

Unfortunately every time they lit the wicks on the metal letters, the 'V' would go out before they could set the last 'E' on fire! The final image might not have blazed quite as it did in their minds but it was still highly effective. And the inside cover shoot of a car on fire was even more dramatic. The band are just lazing around, reading the paper or playing chess in front of a picturesque old-fashioned farmhouse, while behind them a car is apparently exploding.

"I remember that day vividly," says Brian. "I bought a Citroen from this scrapyard in Wigan. It had no MOT on it and it was completely fucked, basically. We bought this car for £50 and it was completely illegal to take it on the road but we ran it up to [Richard's friend] Paul Frodsham's house and we set fire to the fucker, basically. The band were sat around it and Dave Halliwell poured petrol all over it, lit it and nearly killed himself! (laughs uproariously) It was a remarkable day!"

"Richard wanted to set fire to a car," says Michael, "and he had in mind an urban setting for that but I thought it would be a bit obvious, almost making the wrong kind of statement. It was too much of an aggressive image – an urban setting with a car on fire. What's that saying? It was good to juxtapose that against a very rural, peaceful setting. You're getting this ultra violence of the burning car juxtaposed, literally, with this very bucolic, almost like a 19th century, setting.

Basically we had this discussion prior to it of, 'Shall we use diesel or shall we use petrol?' I was very much in the diesel camp because I thought it was more of a viscous liquid and it would burn better and cling to the car better. I lost that argument. But I didn't realise, and nobody realised, that petrol gives off a lot more fumes than diesel and so there was this huge cloud of petrol vapour surrounding the car. Dave Halliwell was in charge of lighting the car with this flintstone style torch. We'd throw some petrol over it, he'd light it, I'd take a few shots with the camera and then the fire would die down and we'd throw some more petrol over it again. So we kept doing this but it was obvious that the car didn't really look on fire so we thought, *Right, let's just completely soak it in petrol*. So then Dave went to light it and he got to within three or four feet and it exploded. Basically it caught fire and the fire went back on to him. It was quite dramatic but we didn't really have much experience of how cars react when you set them on fire. That could have been quite dangerous. It singed his eyebrows I think! It was all caught on film and we watched it but then somebody taped over it later. That was really annoying. We had the whole shoot filmed, including that incident, and then somebody went and taped *Neighbours* over it!

When the fire took hold I'd get the band in for a few seconds and take a few shots and then get them out. Once it got going towards the end, it was literally just a case of getting the band to sit there for a few seconds because things were beginning to burst, tyres were beginning to burst, all these sounds that you'd never heard before. Exploding lightbulbs and things like that. It didn't sound too good. So it was just a case of getting them in quickly and getting them out. In the picture that appeared on the cover, they look very relaxed like they've been there for some time but they've just literally adopted that position. Then a second later they were up again."

By now the band were also putting a similar amount of effort into their videos. Early Verve videos like 'All In The Mind' and 'She's A Superstar' relied on blurry, vaguely psychedelic effects borrowed from the rave scene of the time. To some, it looked as though the directors had just filmed the band when they were seemingly off their faces, with Richard waving his hands portentously in front of his head. For 'Slide Away', the first American single off *A Storm In Heaven*, though, they headed out to a small village called San Jose in Spain.

The director, Richie Smith, had decided that they needed something seedier and darker than their normal setting so he filmed them in a rickety brothel in America, complete with resident prostitutes looking bored in the background. "Those women should have their own TV show," Richard said to *Melody Maker* at the time. "They're stars, they can turn it on every night."

In retrospect, it was a strange decision to choose 'Slide Away' to be the first single for America instead of *Blue*. Perhaps it was because it had more of an 'American' sound, with epic guitars and more of a widescreen feel than the disturbing claustrophobia of 'Blue'. It was also slightly more shoe-gazey, initially, a bit like Ride and maybe that's what the American label expected from British bands at the time.

But, as always with Verve, things didn't go according to plan. Their attempts to conquer America, or at least make a bit of a dent there, were soon threatened by an unlikely source. Jazz label Verve threatened to sue them if they didn't change their name.

"They said someone might go into a record shop and say 'I want a new Verve record' and they'd be given a record by this British pop group when they obviously want a jazz record," says Phill Savidge. "Like most people go into a record shop and say 'I'd like a Sony record please!' There was a point where they were thinking of what to call the band for about a month. Now people don't even know they were called 'Verve' but at the time it felt like a big kick in the teeth."

Rather brilliantly, they talked about simply calling themselves 'Verv' so they could name their next album *Dropping An 'E' For America*, but in the end they simply went for *The* Verve. Bizarre as it might sound now to everybody who knows them as The Verve, this new name took quite some getting used to. When they started the group, it seemed like it was mandatory for every new band to have a one syllable name – Moose, Ride, Lush, Curve, Blur – it was a long time before 'The ...' bands were to return to favour in the early Noughties.

The first release under the new moniker was *The Verve EP* – a five track compilation of slightly truncated versions of their early singles and full length versions of their B-sides for America. It must have been hard for American rock fans to know what to make of them. While Verve were writing their first songs in 1991, Nirvana were totally changing the global music scene. It was, according to the Sonic Youth documentary, *The Year That Punk Broke*. Suddenly bands across the country were chopping off their poodle-perms, buying thrift store lumberjack shirts and playing the sludgey version of punk that was now known as 'grunge'.

But, despite the fact that the old guard of posturing rock stars were supposedly on their way out, the established rules of American music still applied. Everything either rocked or it sucked. *The Verve EP* certainly didn't rock in any conventional sense. 'Endless Life', for example, was seemingly another attempt to soundtrack the sun coming up. Richard is almost whispering, rather than singing and there are no riffs, drums or easily discernible bassline at all for the first three minutes. Instead, Nick lets his guitar create a wash of yearning sound overlaid with occasional sparkles of noise. Gradually the song gets bigger and bigger, a booming rhythm kicking in as Nick starts riffing furiously and Richard howls the title over the top.

Tracks like this and the ten-minute long 'Feel' weren't exactly 'Smells Like Teen Spirit'. Nevertheless there was an audience for what American critics clumsily dubbed 'Dreampop'. Years later, many new bands would rediscover the sound but at the time they merely had an audience among the kind of Anglophiles who eagerly sought out imports of *NME* and *Melody Maker* magazine. This gratifying sense of being in on something a little bit élitist was bolstered by the band's next US release – a live album called *Voyager 1*. Particularly exclusive was the clear blue vinyl version. Only 1000 copies of it were ever made and 300 of these were irreparably damaged in transit from the UK to the US. *Voyager 1* represented the band at their most shoe-gazey (or 'dreampoppy'). Live they drew things out even further than they did on vinyl. It was the kind of record that was never going to be mainstream on either side of the Atlantic but those fans who liked it absolutely loved it. The nature of the music meant that it was designed to be listened to intensely, on headphones if possible and late at night. It wasn't music to stick on while doing the washing up or getting ready to go out. This also meant, of course, that it wasn't music that radio programmers were in a rush to play. They wanted songs that were designed precisely to live in the background of people's lives. This would always limit The Verve's record sales in their early days. Before the internet was commonplace, it was still much harder for music fans to hear obscure sounds, even if they were written about in the music press.

'Blue' didn't do as well as they'd expected, or as well as it deserved, peaking well outside the Top 40 at number 69. The album itself only just made it inside the Top 30. Some reviews complained that it was too dark and obsessed with death but in reality *A Storm In Heaven* exhibited a genuine lust for life in the way that the band dived wholeheartedly into the music. Richard quite liked the idea that they might have scared people a little bit.

"We've always been a dark band, dark in a way that can be quite frightening," he said to *Melody Maker*. "A lot of people heard the first takes of our the album and said, 'You're obsessed with death.' Maybe I am. I think you're a fool if it's not on your mind. My father died when I was eleven. If I died at the same age as my dad, I'd only have eighteen years left. That's terrifying. So that gives you an urgency."

Some reviews were simply ecstatic. In *Alternative Press*, Dave Seagal said, "I've just spent an intense week listening to *A Storm In Heaven* … and I can barely contain my excitement. Not since 1988, when My Bloody Valentine's *Isn't Anything* busted open rock and loosed a new alien magma, have I been so all-fired intoxicated by a piece of music. Unless something extraordinary happens, *A Storm In Heaven* will the best album of 1993."

Others didn't get it at all. *The Sunday Times* complained that, "if you texture and torture the sound to this degree, you begin to convey the impression that you don't believe in the songs; and while there are some rather flimsy wails here, there are also some more robust rockers which don't benefit from carrying this much baggage."

This was kind of missing the point. The "texturing and torturing" of the sound wasn't some kind of add-on to the songs, it was what The Verve did at this point – partly in a bid to escape from producing anything that could remotely be described as a "robust rocker."

Later that summer, they reached another milestone – their first performance at Glastonbury Festival. Richard had never been before and he was eager to see if it would live up to his expectations. Unlike most bands, The Verve didn't just jet in and out, either. They bought tents and stayed for the weekend. And not in the segregated music biz area. "We're not with the people on the hill," Richard joked with MTV interviewer Paul King. "We're with the people over there who couldn't get in with the people on the hill."

Initially things weren't great. The day they were due to perform it was grey and cold. "The way I'd imagined it, it would be 80 degrees, everybody stripped and sweating in the sun," he said. "But instead it's anoraks and shivering."

This was pretty much par for the course for Glastonbury but there was more bad news to come. They were given a slot just before big-hatted jazz-funker Jamiroquai but, before they could play, they had four guitars stolen from their van.

They eventually managed to borrow equipment from another band but that wasn't the end of their difficulties. Nick's amp blew up halfway through one song and they struggled with other technical problems. Despite all this, their performance was everything fans had hoped for. The version of 'Gravity Grave', in particular, sounded absolutely fantastic. Richard stalked the stage in a feral crouch howling the words into the wind as the rest of the band locked into a rolling, crunching groove. They carried on playing for fifteen minutes and eventually had to be forced to leave the stage!

It was a memorable way to regain some of the confidence they might have lost after *A Storm In Heaven*'s poor critical and commercial reception. It was also one small dream of Richard's realised. "I couldn't afford to come to something like this," he told Paul King. "The only chance I'd get to go to a festival was if I was playing in a band."

That version of 'Gravity Grave' was captured forever on the *No Come Down* album, a collection of B-sides and rarities which was their first release as The Verve in the UK. It's stronger and heavier than the single version and it was a pointer towards the new sound they were moving towards with their next studio album.

At this point, while outside forces might occasionally thwart them, their own self-destructive urges were always far more dangerous. They already had a reputation for their partying. As early as 1992, they were banned from the Columbia Hotel in London. A group of friends from Wigan had come down to see them and they managed to persuade the bar manager to stay open by buying him drinks. A few hours later he was reportedly discovered unconscious while the band had borrowed his keys and let themselves in to nose around the most expensive suites upstairs!

It was around this time that the band started to talk about something they called 'The Verve voodoo'. Basically, every time things seemed to be going right, something would go wrong. In 1994, for example, they were forced to cancel their next appearance at Glastonbury after drummer Pete broke his ankle. This time it wasn't an Ashcroft tackle that did it. He got up in the night to get a glass of water and, stumbling around in the dark, walked into a picture frame that was leaning against the wall. It smashed down on his leg and doctors told him it would need to be in plaster for ten weeks to repair the damage. This meant not only missing

Glastonbury but also a gig at the Clapham Grand in London and several US dates. When they did make it out on tour, though, things got even worse.

Richard Ashcroft almost died after a performance on the Lollapalooza tour of America.

CHAPTER 5

CRACKING AMERICA OR CRACKING UP?

Lollapalooza is a tour that traditionally winds its way around America during the summer months. Set up by Perry Farrell of Jane's Addiction, it was intended to be a celebration of alternative music but for many of the bands who played, it often came to seem like one of their toughest gigs. Dinosaur Jr's J Mascis, who played the year before The Verve, remembers how hard it could be.

"I never wanted to do it," he says. "It was like hell. It didn't do any good for our career, it made [Dinosaur Jr's drummer] Murph quit, it totally burnt him out. You only play every three days. If you're on tour and you only play for 45 minutes every three days it's boring. And when we played it was always the hottest day of the year in every town we played in and we played at the hottest time of the day. My amps would always blow up."

The Verve's experience was similar. They were hugely excited to be playing the tour, particularly as the mainstage would see a performance by one of their biggest idols – George Clinton of Parliament and Funkadelic.

"Richard loved [Funkadelic single] 'Funky Dollar Bill' and all that Parliament, Funkadelic sort of stuff," says John Best. "They used to play 'Funky Dollar Bill' in rehearsal – which I used to love."

However, the reality wasn't quite as they'd hoped. "We played the second stage at Lollapalooza, which effectively means you're playing the car park," says John. "They don't have a second stage so it's generally just out the back on a bit of concrete. That's where we were. Us and the Flaming Lips."

They dealt with the boredom in traditional fashion by drinking too much and partying too hard. Every morning Richard would still be up as a group of Tibetan monks blessed the stage and then, still fully robed, tried to get him to join their games of football! The night before they played Kansas, some of the band and John went out drinking while the rest of them stayed in their hotel rooms, also drinking.

"Me and Richard went out," remembers John, "but Richard doesn't really eat. It's very rare to see him eat. So we got off the bus and went to a bar where members of the Bad Seeds and L7 were. You can imagine it was quite alcohol fuelled. We got wasted and then went back to the hotel at half two or three o'clock in the morning. As we arrived, Peter the drummer and our guitar tech were being led away by the police in handcuffs because they'd decided that they'd chuck the furniture out of the window.

We were really drunk and not in the right frame of mind to deal with the situation. Not much sleep was had as a result. Then we got bail and got Pete out and by the time they played it was about 110 degrees, middle of the summer in the middle of America, just stupidly hot. We played at about one o'clock in the full heat of the day with the sun shining directly on to the stage."

The gig itself went well but even on-stage Richard was already starting to feel bad. "I'd been drinking for the last three weeks on the road," he told Robert Cherry of *Alternative Press* afterwards. "There were bands on the Main Stage who didn't touch the rider, so I'd be infiltrating their tents and drinking it for them."

The real problems occurred when he got off-stage and looked at The Verve's guitar roadie. He had a massive cut on his leg which he hadn't bothered to put any kind of bandage or plaster on. The sight of it made Richard start to feel very ill.

"He started going (breathing heavily) 'I feel really weird,'" remembers John Best. "'OK, you're probably dehydrated, have some water.' So we got him some water. Then he started going (moans) 'I really don't feel well.' I started to take him seriously because he'd gone ashen. So I ran to the catering staff and said 'My singer's got heat exhaustion. I need a paramedic.' But could we get a fucking paramedic? They were radioing people and it took about fifteen minutes. By then we'd taken him to a dark room and laid him down and covered him with ice.

Me and [music journalist] Ann Scanlon did actually think he might die, because there's a point with heat exhaustion where your blood vessels burst and horrible things start to happen. He was properly delirious. Eventually an ambulance came, about half an hour after he said he was unwell, and as soon as he got in the ambulance they put a drip in his arm. I went with him in the ambulance to the hospital and they said he was something between 60 and 70 percent dehydrated. I don't know what that means. It was very dangerous. It was quite scary."

As he was carried into the ambulance, despite being so ill, Richard gave the waiting photographers a thumbs up. "There's a scene in *The Simpsons* when the stunt rider guy does his jump over the shark pool, puts his thumb up and then he falls in," he explained to *Q*. "It was like 'Yeah, kids, Evel Knievel's alright.'"

When he got to the hospital, though, he was quickly made aware of how serious the situation was. "I thought I was gonna die," he continued. "I had some mad doctor holding me cock while I was trying to pee in a bottle and two drips coming out of me arms … I know now I'm really lucky I didn't die."

Luckily he recovered quickly and the damage Pete caused to the hotel room only came to $450. Nevertheless they were still getting a reputation as rock 'n' roll casualties. "Did you see Verve?" quipped Kim Deal of The Breeders. "You better go see them quick, before they all die."

Against doctor's orders, Richard played again the next night, with the marks from where the saline drip had been removed still visible on his arm. Possibly the next dates suffered. *Melody Maker's* reviewer was highly scathing. "The Verve are a collective crap Jesus," they sniped. "It makes us embarrassed to be British. They're so fake, so transparent, so lacking in substance."

"No wonder we went a bit mad on Lollapalooza," Richard said to *Guitar* magazine's Dan Eccleston, "if you could get us a room full of instruments, a PA and a bit of draw, then we'd be in there jamming. Instead you wake up in a car park outside some Superbowl stadium 25 miles from anywhere, where there's nothing to do but drink. It would get to anyone, that.'"

Still, Lollapalooza was the point at which Richard pulled back from the brink. "I don't wanna go there again," he said. "It doesn't make you wary, really, it just makes you realise that when you're young, you don't know how far you can take it until you realise your limits … your physical and mental limits."

The band's reputation as hellraisers was further enhanced by their association with another young gang – Oasis. In 1993, The Verve's sleeve designer Brian Cannon bumped into a young roadie – Noel Gallagher. At the time Brian's design company Microdot shared its offices with the Inspiral Carpets and Noel Gallagher worked for them. "He said this guy he met in a lift, who had nice trainers and a good haircut, gave him a really strong demo," Richard said in a radio interview with Clint Boon.

But, according to Brian Cannon, the alliance between two of the most successful British bands of the Nineties was encouraged by his decision to take his mother on holiday. "I took her to Rome for her 60th birthday because she's a big Catholic," he says, "and while we were there I bought these astonishing Adidas trainers which you couldn't get over here. I'd seen Noel around for a while but we were getting the lift one day and the first words Noel Gallagher ever said to me were 'Alright, I put my hands up, where did you get those fucking trainers?'

"I said 'I took my mum to Rome.' He said 'What do you do?' I said I design record sleeves for The Verve. He said 'No way! What have you done?' Well, I'd only done two singles by that point. He said: 'Right, I'm getting a band together and I want you to do my artwork.' That's quite literally how I ended up working with Oasis as well."

But, before that, Brian played the dcmo to Richard Ashcroft who could hardly believe what he was hearing, particularly the eventual classic 'Live Forever'. "The lyric I heard immediately made me want to cry, it's such a beautiful, innocent song," he said. "From the moment I heard it I thought, *This is going to be outrageous.*"

"That's how the Verve–Oasis coalition came about," says Brian. "Noel Gallagher gave me that tape and I played it to Richard Ashcroft and rock 'n' roll history was therefore made. It was fucking unbelievable. The two best rock 'n' roll bands in the world and I was working with both of them. It was fucking mega."

Before anyone had heard of the Mancunians, The Verve took them on tour. There were a few other bands they got on well with, but in Oasis they felt like they'd found kindred spirits. After a power-cut in Glasgow, Richard, Noel Gallagher and Nick McCabe even performed 'She'll Be Coming Round The Mountain' with Bonehead on spoons!

Richard was surprised and disappointed, though, to see that many of their fans showed little interest in the support band. "It was strange to hear a band play the whole of *Definitely Maybe* to three blokes in tracksuits in Glasgow and then a year later the rest is history," he said. The alliance between Richard Ashcroft and Oasis would ultimately last longer than The Verve themselves. Long after he'd gone solo, Richard would still regard Liam in particular as one of the only people in the world who knew what it was like to be in his position. "Somebody like Liam's an island," he once said. "When I meet him at things like the Q Awards it's like, 'Thank God you're here, mate!'"

After Lollapalooza, The Verve and Oasis went on tour in Europe and found themselves on the front page of Swedish newspapers. The two bands had reportedly gone back to their hotel after the Hultsfred Festival and ended up wrecking the bar, causing £1000 of damage. There was talk that they would be banned from Sweden for life.

However, John Best believes that many of the stories about The Verve in those days were exaggerated. "There was a lot of mythologising the band," he says. "I think because of the way Richard looked, everybody assumed he was hardcore but as far as I remember on tour it was just blasting music and knocking back a couple of bottles of beer. There weren't any alcoholics."

Still, there's no denying that, in 1994 and 1995, tensions were growing within The Verve. It can't have helped that their friends Oasis seemed to be effortlessly achieving the world-conquering status that Richard had always dreamed about. *A Storm In Heaven*, meanwhile, flopped badly.

In one sense, the two bands' methods were converging. Oasis hired Brian Cannon to design the sleeve for their debut album and named one of their songs 'Slide Away'. Meanwhile, The Verve decided that *Definitely Maybe* producer Owen Morris should take control of their next record. But, commercially, they were poles apart. *Definitely Maybe* was far more successful than *A Storm In Heaven* and *(What's The Story) Morning Glory?* was about to send Oasis into the stratosphere.

"It's a lottery, music," says Simon Clarke. "Sometimes it happens, sometimes it doesn't happen. When we worked with The Verve the first time, I thought that they were enormously talented and I did expect that first album to do more. I really thought that would have a massive impact and I was surprised when it didn't. I wasn't surprised when they had success later."

Post-*Definitely Maybe*, the expectations for what an 'indie' band should sell had suddenly escalated and, to some observers, perhaps The Verve were lucky not to be dropped. Brian Cannon believes that it was the continuing support of Dave Boyd that saved them. "He was the man who gave the band the opportunity and, not only that, other labels would have dropped a band who'd spent so much on on the first album and [sold] fuck all. But David Boyd was a *believer*."

"It was an extraordinary time," says John Best. "It went from My Bloody Valentine being the pinnacle of artistic endeavour to bands just selling phenomenal amounts of records. A lot of people had their eyes on the prize."

One significant change in the mid-Nineties was that Radio One suddenly started playing guitar music again. When Blur released their first song that you could describe as Britpop, 'For Tomorrow', it barely received any airplay. Their halcyon days as a southern response to Madchester seemed to be far behind them. Fast forward to *Parklife* and suddenly they were everywhere. Ironically, despite having been around before most of the Britpop bands, The Verve only reaped the benefits of the changing climate much later.

In 1994 the Verve voodoo was still in full effect. At a gig in Paris with Oasis, Nick lost his backstage pass and got into an altercation with a security guard who wouldn't let him back in the building. He ended up being punched and kicked down some concrete steps, breaking a finger in the process and having to cancel a month's dates. Around the same time, an even more painful fate was about to befall Richard Ashcroft. Sarah, his girlfriend of six years broke up with him. He hinted in interviews that she'd left him for a mutual friend.

It was a huge blow. Even Oasis were worried about him and, as a tribute and a wake-up call, Noel wrote 'Cast No Shadow' about his friend. "It's a big deal to people because it's on a huge Oasis album,"

Richard said to *The Scotsman*. "But I think Noel would have done it even if they were selling 400 copies. It's something between me and Noel. It touched me, simple as that, it is a beautiful song and at the same time it was quite relevant to me. Oasis are honest. They make soul music. It's coming from Noel and the band's hearts."

Richard took the song as it was intended, as a compliment, but he was slightly confused by the lyric. He suggested in one interview that Noel must think he was "like Dracula".

"I always interpreted it in the most literal way," says John Best, "that he was so skinny he cast no shadow! But he definitely looked at Oasis, who had supported him, and thought 'I want that, I really want that!'"

Nevertheless, despite Oasis being one of the biggest bands in the world, The Verve's position in the rock hierarchy was confirmed by their billing at 1994's Reading Festival where *Melody Maker* memorably likened Richard Ashcroft to a "preying mantis high on Anadin." They were on the mainstage, but very early on the Friday. They were above cult band Flaming Lips but below the relatively obscure Trans-Global Underground, Gang Starr and six other bands, including Cypress Hill who were headlining.

It was a strange year for rock. Just a few months previously Kurt Cobain had killed himself but his wife's band, Hole, were already back, playing on the same day as The Verve. Courtney Love said that she wanted her performance to be seen as a tribute to her husband but it was shambolic and distressing as she struggled to keep it together. On the same night, the rambling, dishevelled appearance of Lemonheads' singer Evan Dando made some observers think that he was in danger of going the same way as Kurt. Then, on the Saturday night, the Manic Street Preachers were forced to play their first festival performance as a three-piece. Bass player Richey Edwards was in rehab and he, too, would be missing within the year.

The rock casualty list at the time must have given many stars pause for thought, but it didn't seem to slow The Verve down. The combination of heartache, more free time and a burning desire to emulate his former protégés would spur Richard Ashcroft and The Verve on to their biggest change of direction yet. It would also precipitate a colossal drugs binge which would almost cost them their minds and contribute to the eventual break-up of the band.

CHAPTER 6

NORTHERN SOULS

Nick McCabe would later describe the first three weeks of recording The verve's second album, *A Northern Soul*, as one of the best times of his life. The whole process was certainly among the most intense experiences of all of their lives. When they were making *A Storm In Heaven*, they had few responsibilities and just went into the studio with John Leckie, smoked spliffs and waited to see what would turn up. Less than two years later, Nick's relationship with the mother of his newborn child was fragmenting, Richard's had split up with his girlfriend, Simon had got married and suddenly Britpop had made 'indie' an enormous business.

Determined not to make the same mistakes they had with *A Storm In Heaven*, they tried to write before going into the studio. They booked their old rehearsal room in Wigan, "a black hole, a claustrophobic pit," as Richard described it, and got straight down to work. It was a decision of calculated masochism. They were still mentally and physically exhausted from the summer's tours. To compensate they tried to make sense of the chaos in their personal lives through the music.

"When you come home after you've been through all the madness, that was difficult to deal with," Simon Jones said to *Melody Maker*'s Dave Simpson. "You're drained by America and then you come back to this 'real' environment that's supposed to be your life but you don't know who you are. You don't know whether you're the person you were on tour or the person back at home."

Sometimes they'd just drive around at night waiting for inspiration to come. However, before they could get going, Richard went to try and sort things out with Sarah in London. He was gone for three months.

"Things didn't go so well," he understated to *Detour* magazine, "and I got really fucked up for about two of those months, both physically and mentally. When I got back, the strangest thing was that they were playing music that was precisely the way I was feeling and so the two just went together quite easily."

At one of their rehearsal sessions, they invited producer Owen Morris along to listen. Owen Morris was still relatively inexperienced compared with John Leckie but his reputation had been given a massive boost after he was judged by some to have 'rescued' *Definitely Maybe*. The recording sessions for Oasis's debut album had already been through the hands of two producers and taken in numerous studios but Noel Gallagher was still unhappy with the results. He had tried to beef things up by layering on guitar overdubs but the band and Creation Records' boss Alan McGee still didn't like what they were hearing. Owen had worked as an engineer for several years but he'd never produced, nevertheless they decided to give him a chance. He stripped away most of the overdubs but made the record sound much louder than it had previously. When *Definitely Maybe* became the fastest selling debut album of all-time in the UK, he duly took a small part of the credit.

He later said that The Verve "just blew my head off" during those early sessions. The original plan was to record the album in Wigan but, instead, they decamped to Loco Studios in south Wales. "When we got them to Loco studios," he said later, "my task was to capture, basically, the sound of them just playing together and not to bland it out by trying to be too clever."

That makes it all sound very simple but the way they made the record was highly unorthodox. They created a kind of club vibe in the studio, listening to music all the time, taking ecstasy and just banging out tunes when inspiration struck them. "It was just like doing a gig," Simon Jones said. "We didn't have to worry about anything but getting off our heads and playing music.

The euphoric, successful first weeks of recording at Loco were at least partly fuelled by large quantities of ecstasy. They weren't far from Newport, which Nick McCabe describes as the drug capital of Wales and some reports suggest they took E every day for the first three weeks. After the high, though, there was an inevitable comedown.

"There are things that have gone on in The Verve that I won't be talking about in this interview and I won't be talking about until the day I die," Richard said to Paul Moody of *Dazed and Confused* in 1997. "If we were an American band, I might talk about them and go on to sell 15 million albums on the back of it, but because we're from Wigan, and we all love each other, we're not gonna start talking about it. Let's just say there was a cloud over us."

The stories of what went on at Loco would become legendary – to quote John Best, it was like "the fucking lunatics taking over the asylum"; for his part, Owen found the experience just as draining as the band did. "They don't really need a producer,' he said to *Guitar Magazine*, "because they will do [a] producer's head in. They did my head in, completely and utterly. There you go. That's life. It's a fantastic album at the end of the day, but it's not a process that I'd ever want to go through again, ha ha!"

Richard Ashcroft was hugely impressed that Owen Morris was prepared to commit himself to their recordings with the same intensity as the rest of the band, almost acting like a fifth member. For Nick McCabe, though, after the first three weeks, things started to become a little sinister. He was very down because of problems with his girlfriend. The constant partying and need to be 'up' began to seem oppressive.

"I remember going to Loco," says John, "and Richard, who didn't have a driving license, had been driving a car round and round on the lawn and he'd gone up the curb and taken the tyre off the wheel hub so there were big gouge marks where he was driving the car without a tyre on the wheel!"

"If we don't reach that level of inspiration then we don't play," Richard said to *Guitar* magazine. "We go down the pub instead … if you take a photograph of four people, the chances that all four are going to look good at that single moment in time are a million to one. And it's the same when four people pick up instruments at the same time."

The rest of the band were happy to go along with the partying but Nick started to find the experience increasingly difficult. "Nick was introspective," says John. "Richard was like the ring-leader and Simon and Sobbo were happy to smoke dope. I think Nick was aware that he was more delicate. He didn't have the robust constitution of the others. He was given to dark thoughts. He avoided intense dope-smoking sessions or getting absolutely wankered. By the time I got to Loco, they were almost on different clocks. Richard and the rest of the band would want to get up about two and start recording after dinner at about six o'clock and then go to bed at six the next morning. Nick had a child so he wanted to go to work at about ten or eleven in the morning and finish at ten or eleven at night."

"I was a total emotional wreck," Nick told *The Face*. "It got to the point that all I had in common with the rest of them was the music. My home life was a disaster and I didn't feel comfortable anywhere."

They realised eventually that they were only ever getting anything done on Wednesdays. They would take three days to build up to a peak and then spend the next three days coming down. When they weren't laying down tracks, they would listen to music, smoke weed, take ecstasy and jam endlessly. The fact that out of this process special moments occurred made it all seem worthwhile but the intense nature of the sessions started to take their toll. Ironically, part of the problem came from Richard's increasing confidence in his songwriting. He was still happy to provide vocals over tracks already laid down by the rest of the band but, after the split with Sarah, he'd also written very different songs himself.

"When Sarah and Richard eventually split-up, Richard became peripatetic – semi-homeless," John Best says. "To his credit he was pretty good at it. In those days he didn't really need or have anything. He'd come and see us and he didn't have money for a ticket so he'd bunk on the train and stay in the toilet the whole way down. Then he'd come and see me with no money and no socks on his feet. He had jeans, a t-shirt and maybe a jacket and that'd be it. He didn't have any money and he didn't have any clothes but he still had the rock star bearing."

At the time John was going out with Miki Berenyi of Lush and, for six to eight weeks, Richard came to stay with them. "We had a portastudio in the front room that Miki had for writing her songs on," John continues, "and he had nothing to do all day so he'd sit in our frontroom with her acoustic guitar just writing songs. As far as I know it was the first time he'd had time on his own to really work any of this stuff out.

That's why on *A Northern Soul* there are two records fighting each other. There's *A Storm In Heaven* and [third album] *Urban Hymns* and they come together on that. You've got songs that are traditional Verve psychedelic work-outs and then you've got songs like 'History' that I heard and thought, *Wow! This is a very interesting new development.*"

For all the problems that they had, everybody who visited the studios, including the Gallaghers, were astonished by the music they were hearing. Miles Leonard says that, despite the chaos, he wasn't worried about them because they were clearly being so productive.

"Ultimately the songs were coming through," he says. "I remember going down to Loco and being in there and realising that here was a band that were in the throes of excess. They were on the brink of collapsing or damaging themselves but at the same time hearing songs like 'A New Decade' or 'History' – you just heard that tension, almost darkness that was there. There were the classic highs and lows of a really drugged-up session and that was reflected in the music.

It was incredibly dark and powerful and direct. It was just an amazing album. The combination between them and Owen Morris worked in so many ways but it had that recreational effect as well – the same as it probably did for Oasis. I think they fed off each other. He was controlling and encouraging everything that was going on.

There was a real sense of them, not winding each other up, but there was just this tension building in the room which was explosive. There was just this sense of excitement about how great the record was. They didn't have a care in the world apart from what they were doing."

"When I went to the playback to hear what they'd been doing, I walked into this mayhem," says John Best. "The music was ear-splittingly loud, almost on the verge of pain and Owen Morris was going (arms aloft) 'Listen to fucking this!' He got on this chair and walked on to the desk with all these delicate little dials and he was standing on it with a vodka and tonic in his hand and it was in a straight glass with a heavy bottom. He got it and chucked it across the room at the studio glass. It's reinforced glass and he chucked it so hard that it went 'Smash!' That was about one and a half grand's worth of glass that we had to pay for!

Honestly, I found the machismo a little repellent. My perspective was that it was the time of the Gallaghers and there was something of that creeping in that I didn't like or want to be part of. It was the first time that I felt a little bit outside of the process. I liked the music but I thought it was getting a bit laddy."

This was the new spirit of the age, however. The Nineties was the time of the "new lad" with *Loaded* magazine launching in 1994 and football terrace culture still reaching new heights in the wake of the 1990 World Cup. Things had changed massively since *A Storm In Heaven* where Verve's sound at times bordered on fey. Although there was still a major element of Richard's personality that was the hippy 'student' of Brian Cannon's description, there was also a new aggression that came out in the music and their behaviour.

"We needed a producer who would be extreme," Richard said later. "Owen brought his personality to the record. He's the only person I know who can smash a thirty foot window in the studio and then do his job. He admitted he nearly had a nervous breakdown, and I think that's a commendable performance."

When they released the first single from those sessions, 'This Is Music', that belligerent spirit was immediately very apparent. Instead of singing vague platitudes about the sky and the sun, as he had in the past, Richard was suddenly addressing the real world. He'd met somebody who went to expensive public school Eton and that provided the song's striking opening line – a cry of defiance, rather than complaint – about the fact that he'd been born without a "silver spoon."

"I just realised the options that were open to him if he wanted to venture into certain fields," Richard told Dave Simpson of *Melody Maker*. "He was 90 metres ahead in the race of life, purely by birth right. And I find that really strange. So I invented a character with which to sing the song. But it could be me, easily. Or anyone who's been into a situation where you have to fight to get what you want."

The influence of Oasis or, more to the point, Liam Gallagher, is highly evident in 'This Is Music'. The vocals are suddenly right at the top of the mix, totally confident, bordering on arrogant. All of a sudden The Verve seem like Richard Ashcroft's band as much as Nick McCabe's. However loud the guitars get, his voice always dominates right up to the final, defiant lyric. It's also a song about

Richard's life in a way that previous songs hadn't been. As well as the opening lines about class, it also delves with new honesty into his feelings about being single for the first time after his six-year relationship had ended. All his private insecurity is evident in the lyrics and yet by the time they were recorded, a drug-fuelled bravado has entered the mix. Richard was often reluctant when questioned in interviews to give Sarah any credit for inspiring *A Northern Soul* and you can hear in the way he sings the lyric that he's far from wallowing in misery.

It was the second single, 'On Your Own', where he reveals some vulnerability for the first time. It was The Verve's first ballad and at the time it seemed like a rare oddity, but it would ultimately seem like a pointer towards their later style. To Richard, the fact that he could write something like that, without quite so much input from the rest of the band, was a revelation. "When I first heard it," he said in a video interview with *Planet Rock*, "I played it 35 times on a little tape recorder to myself back in the room. I couldn't believe how it started and had a middle and an end and it all seemed balanced and clear and crystal. That was a great moment."

Although Richard's vocal is uncharacteristically shaky, you can hear in the falsetto chorus that he's starting to measure himself, not against other indie bands, but against great soul singers like Al Green. There's little room for Nick's characteristic effects-drenched guitar sound. Instead the rest of the band are there to provide a backdrop to the vocal. Nick's greatness as a guitarist comes from the way that he uses the instrument almost like other musicians would use a synthesiser. He doesn't care all that much about technical virtuosity in the traditional sense. Instead he uses the guitar as a way to create sounds that he then manipulates, distorts and controls with the effects pedals. There was no room for that on 'On Your Own'. The vocal is suddenly demanding all the space that Nick used to occupy and the most distinctive 'effect' is the tinkling piano that comes in towards the end. Where The Verve used to see their role models as being bands like Can, who'd never sought out mainstream success, they were now aiming for something closer to classic rock.

Richard was undoubtedly right that this had much greater popular appeal. While *A Storm In Heaven* only struck a nerve with the kind of people who listen to music intently, over and over again, the new songs he was starting to write were far more direct. Casual listeners could relate to the strong melody and raw soul-baring in a way that they couldn't to the spaciness of the earlier Verve singles. 'On Your Own' didn't perfect the formula but it was a step in the direction of Oasis's globe-straddling ubiquity.

But although the singles provided one vision of the band, there was a lot more to *A Northern Soul* than the singles. For about ten seconds the album sounds a bit like *A Storm In Heaven*. Opening track 'A New Decade' fades up slowly with Richard woo-woohing gently somewhere far off in the distance. Then, suddenly, the guitars kick the metaphorical doors in and Richard bellows the title like he's announcing the start of a whole new era. The most noticeable change is that the vocals are far higher in the mix than they were before and the guitars are angrier and heavier. It's still space-rock but it's *Star Wars* rather than *2001: A Space Odyssey*.

And if that seemed like a statement of intent, 'This Is Music' was a full-on manifesto, albeit of a crazed, incoherent kind. It starts with a rattlesnake shake of maracas and then Richard launches into his urgent, impassioned rant about the class system and, perhaps more importantly, the fact that he didn't have a girlfriend. There are highs and lows just as there were on *A Storm In Heaven* but the highs, unsurprisingly considering their drug intake, are much higher. It sounds like Owen Morris has got them to turn everything up to 11, including Richard's larynx. It's not hard to understand why he felt the need to smash something when he heard the finished version for the first time. Nick had come up with an extraordinary guitar sound from a cheap, cast aluminium guitar from the early Eighties. It only had three strings and it was completely out of tune giving the riff a harsh, metallic sound which fitted perfectly with the brutal music.

Even Richard was blown away when he first heard what Nick, Simon and Pete had come up with. "I came back and heard 'This Is Music' he said to *Planet Rock*, "and it was 35 minutes long. It was Funkadelic. It was Jimi Hendrix. It was incredible. There was a chance there to bring it together and make it into an explosive song."

It was through doing that kind of arrangement work that Richard first realised that he was a songwriter. It taught him where the chorus should go and how to write something that was dangerously close to a 'pop song'. 'This Is Music' was one of those occasions when The Verve found the perfect balance between Richard's desire to express himself simply and clearly and the band's love of psychedelia, noise and chaos.

That's why 'On Your Own' must have come as a huge shock for fans expecting more of the same. It's The Verve as millions would come to know them in the future – writers of ballads designed to make the world cry. Without Nick's guitar fireworks it's all about Richard's voice and Richard's feelings. The mixture between tracks like that and 'So It Goes', which harked back to *A Storm In Heaven*, gave *A Northern Soul* a very uneven feel. It's not an album that flows smoothly. Undoubtedly many people who bought the record after hearing 'History' would have skipped right past 'So It Goes'. It starts like Oasis and carries on with the same refrain as 'On Your Own' but set against mellow guitars this time. It sounds like Richard's improvising just like he did on *A Storm In Heaven* but the crucial difference is that this time you can hear every word he sings as he bemoans his love life and the inevitability of dying alone.

It doesn't work as well as similar tracks on their debut and its deficiencies are more noticeable because of the great songs on either side. For example, the title track is an incredible piece of music with some of the oddest guitar sounds that Nick has ever produced. With the addition of keyboards from Simon, it manages the unique trick of sounding utterly rock 'n' roll without having any recognisably rock 'n' roll riffs, structure or melody. It could be the Chemical Brothers slowed down to a mighty crawl. By the end, as the guitar morphs into seagull noises, you can almost hear the euphoria of the initial recording sessions changing into a disturbing psychosis, but it still carries an incredible charge.

From then on, the energy level of the record changes. Track six – 'Brainstorm Interlude' – is the sound of the band boiling over and freaking out. There are great moments but they're bobbing in a sea of frantic noodling. It sounds like they were jamming to try and find a song, one didn't appear but the resulting chaos was too good to ignore.

In comparison the next track, 'Drive You Home', is pure balm – a gentle, country ballad, a second cousin to 'See You In The Next

One (Have A Good Time)' It's a slow, sleepy tune and not at all bad, but it goes on for far too long, perhaps suggesting to some that they might be running out of ideas. There's no indication at all of what would come next – the beautiful strings and career high point vocals of 'History'.

'History' doesn't sound like it belongs on *A Northern Soul* – it would have made more sense on the follow-up album, *Urban Hymns*, but it's none the worse for that despite being the last genuinely great moment on the album and, eventually, the first unequivocally classic single The Verve ever released.

But, by the next track, 'No Knock On My Door', Richard is sounding more like Liam Gallagher than he ever had before. You can almost imagine him standing slightly too far from the mic, leaning over it with his hands behind his back, shouting to make himself heard. The machismo that John Best talked about is in full-effect but you can hear him expending his last drop of strength.

For the last few tracks the energy levels plummet. 'Life's An Ocean' is a song about feeling drained and listless and that, despite the excellent lyric and a bassline of Pacific depth, is the way it sounds. 'Stormy Clouds' summons up the same mood but much more effectively, drifting in a dreamlike fashion before the rhythm section subtly accelerates, pulling the song forward like a tractor dragging a sports car off a muddy field. The theme continues with 'Reprise' – several minutes of noodling, essentially, that proves the point that the shattered band seemed to have absolutely no idea how to finish the fantastic work they'd started.

As a whole, *A Northern Soul* wasn't as coherent an album as *A Storm In Heaven* but its best moments would be among the best moments of 1995. They'd flown far away from their roots in obscure space rock and now they had songs that they could proudly put alongside the classic tunes of their youth.

This comes across on the sleeve of *A Northern Soul*. Brian Cannon's grandiose cover photo speaks volumes about the band's new ambition. There were echoes of the classic *With The Beatles* album in its centrepiece of four heads against a black background. In the corner was a small door, perhaps representing the door into their minds. They shot the image in a warehouse near Tower Bridge, projecting a picture of the band sixteen metres high against a wall and taking the picture as Sobbo walked through the door.

"I'm a massive Beatles fan," Brian says of the similarity. "But some people say it's almost like a 'Bohemian Rhapsody' thing. Again, we never did anything digitally. We shot them in the studio, wrapped around in black velvet so you could see nothing bar their heads, and then we took that image and projected it against a wall that was used by the [TV programme] *London's Burning* crew. It was mad being in there that day with this literally 50-foot-high image of their heads. If you look at the bottom you see Peter Salisbury walking through the door. We just loved testing ourselves if you like, just like the band did."

But the problem was that the tests the band had put themselves through had become too much for them to take.

CHAPTER 7

HISTORY

To most people, *A Northern Soul* would later be memorable for one song only – the brilliant 'History'. It was the moment The Verve took a giant step towards popular acclaim but it was also symbolic – in more ways than one – of a band that were falling apart. Richard was starting to discover himself as a songwriter and the rest of the band could have been forgiven for thinking they were now almost surplus to requirements as he came up with the initial germ of the idea.

"I went into the studio with two scraps of information, one line of a William Blake poem and a little bit of a melody," Richard said to Radio DJ Gary Crowley of that song. "At three in the morning, I decided to try and record this and the whole six and a half minutes came out as one big flow, like a stream of consciousness, which amazed me. I didn't have to change anything."

In his excitement, as the bones of the song came together, Richard ended up working all night. At six o'clock in the morning he was momentarily jolted from his concentration by the sound of a gardener arriving outside, shaking something in a matchbox. "I dragged him in, this little Welsh gardener," he said to Gary, "'you've got to come and play on this!' So somewhere on there is the gardener!"

'History' marked a turning point for the band. It was the first time they used the lush strings that would be one of the biggest selling points on their most successful records. For that they owed a debt to string arranger extraordinaire Wil Malone. Wil was once best known as a member of psychedelic Sixties band Orange Bicycle and then as the composer of the soundtrack to cult horror film *Death Line*. However, in the Nineties his wonderful string arrangements on Massive Attack's 'Unfinished Sympathy' had given him a whole new kudos. For a time, his strings, or strings in his style, became almost a cliché as grubby indie bands sought them out for a touch of class. They worked brilliantly on 'History' but Nick McCabe had some reservations. He would later complain that the strings were too "posh."

This feeling must have been exacerbated by the fact that, after Loco, Richard headed to London's most famous studio, Abbey Road, to record them. There, along with Liam Gallagher and about 30 other friends, they also recorded the song's handclaps. It was a euphoric moment but for the four-man unit that had been The Verve, the end was rapidly approaching.

"There were two very different people in the band," says John Best. "Richard's got a very powerful ego and Nick's got a very fragile ego. It didn't sit very well together. I think Nick started to be not included on songs. I think he started to think *I don't wanna be in this band* very quickly."

Even when the sessions were finished and Nick went back to stay with his mum in Wigan, he was still in a state of depression and spent much of the time in his room. "My mum was telling me I was psychotic and I needed help from the doctor," he told *The Face*. "She'd be shouting 'What's wrong with you? What's wrong with you?' Then she'd go out and I'd be throwing chairs around, smashing things up."

Richard was suffering the ill-effects of their drug intake. "I didn't feel too good," he admitted to Sylvia Patterson in *The Guardian*. "Just psychosis." "It was a period of extremes," he said to *Q* magazine. "and I suppose the tail end of that was my lowest point. Lowest point mentally. The psychosis, I've had it all. I've seen visions come out of nowhere, I've been Syd Barrett, lying in my sleeping bag in the recording studio. And I'm glad I've been there really. At the time, it frightens the life out of you because once you lose that control over your thought processes to that extent, you're fucked, man. But if you're caning anything, you're gonna get to the point where the demons come and I was seeing the fucking demons."

Michael Spencer Jones: "I think around *Northern Soul* Richard got a bit of a phone phobia," he says. "There was a period when nobody could get in touch with him, record company, anybody. It wasn't too obvious that they had problems. I never really saw any friction although I heard about situations that had gone on. They always managed to get it together when they played live."

John Best says that he could see there were serious problems during the *A Northern Soul* sessions. "I was worried about the band," he says. "Young men in general, in bands especially, don't communicate very well. If they've got a problem they tend to bottle it up. I went to Simon's wedding when he got married to an American girl he met on Lollapalooza. After the wedding, all the men were down one end playing fruit machines and all the women were down the other end talking to each other. They're very taciturn Northern boys. I could see that there was a problem and I could see that they weren't talking about it."

"I could see Richard becoming more insular during that time," says Phill Savidge. "He was becoming separate from the rest of the band because he was being singled out by the music press and obviously he's a great frontman so other people were noticing him and befriending him. As well as Oasis and Spiritualized befriending him, other people were, too. When I think of Richard, I just think of the word 'music' because he used to reek of it!"

'This Is Music' was The Verve's first single in eighteen months and they had high hopes. In the press, it briefly gave them a new image as a 'political' band. It was a label that Richard was reluctant to accept but he was starting to take more of an interest in what was going on around him. "I love England," he said to *Melody Maker*. "But when you analyse it, it's totally fucked. We've had dickheads in power for so long. The Eighties were a terrible, greedy decade. The wrong people making ridiculous amounts of money."

The song made it very clear they weren't the hippies that they'd been pigeon-holed as but not everyone appreciated the belligerent self-belief that their music radiated. *Melody Maker*'s singles reviewer Cathy Unsworth said: "Mad Richard stands at the top of a cliff, arms outstretched. All around him, The Verve's music resounds with the overblown grandeur of the wild and desolate landscape that surrounds him. Jump, you fucker, jump."

She had a point about the song's enormous confidence in its own power but, buried underneath that, of course, were lyrics which explicitly detailed Richard's insecurity and loneliness. It was a misunderstanding of his essential character that would frustrate him throughout his career. He thought people would recognise all the different sides to him that came out in the various songs.

"Lyrically, the whole album is me asking myself: 'Who the fuck am I?'" he said in an interview with *Alternative Press*. "Am I the guy in 'This Is Music' standing tall in the world with these huge guitars around him like the king of rock 'n' roll, or am I the guy in *A Northern Soul* who's wasted and desperate, or am I the guy in 'On Your Own', who's in between life and death, or am I the guy in 'Life's An Ocean' imagining the future and buying feelings from a vending machine, am I this future shock guy?' But I'm all of them, you see. It's dangerous to fracture your personality too much, but that's what it was."

As he'd put it later, he was a million different people, from one day to the next. But, when 'This Is Music' came out and peaked at number 35, it's safe to say that one of his less confident personae probably surfaced. 'On Your Own' did a bit better, but still only reached number 28. Again, not exactly the life-changing result that they'd expected from the sheer effort they'd put into the recordings.

Curiously the lyric garnered some comparisons with the angst-rock gestating on the other side of the Atlantic. One review which compared The Verve's new direction to Pearl Jam particularly infuriated Richard. "The character who's singing that song is way more messed up than [Pearl Jam singer] Eddie Vedder's ever been," he said to *NME*. "But at the end of the song he looks around and says 'I'm too busy staying alive. Too busy living. There's got to be a blue horizon. There's got to be hope.' We've been given too much angst-ridden shit from America for too long. I'm sick of hearing these upper middle-class white boys whining about shit I can't relate to. Just sick."

Despite this repudiation of the sickness that had infected the grunge scene after Kurt Cobain's death, one by-product of the single was a new false rumour about Richard, stemming from the B-side 'Dance On Your Bones', which was about heroin. Richard admitted that he'd encountered the drug, but only vicariously through friends using it.

"Let them say what they want," he said to *Vox* of the rumours surrounding him. "Rumours go around me anyway, I think because

I'm quite a private person, we don't play the scene, never have done, so people will never truly get it. And that's the way I want it. I don't want people to understand it … every fucker seems to be coming back with a distress story, and with us there's no distress anymore."

"A lot of people assumed he was a drug addict, a heroin addict even [because he was so thin]," says John Best. "I firmly believe he never used heroin. Some bands who had cleaner cut images than The Verve were doing more drugs than they ever did."

Richard unequivocally denied that he'd ever used heroin. "I've always understood that, to put my personality in the womb and comfort it from any thoughts of fear, y'know, worry or anxiety, would be like, putting me in a coffin," he told Sylvia Patterson in *The Guardian*.

The first indication for many fans of The Verve's new direction came when they supported Oasis at a filmed gig at Southend's Cliffs Pavilion. The show caught them in belligerent form, with much less of the star sailing of their early days. For the first time since their early singles, a few critics even started predicting that they would become massive again.

A Northern Soul did well, it sold more in its first month than *A Storm In Heaven* had in two years, peaking at number 13, but it didn't reach the stellar heights the band had hoped. In retrospect, it's surprising the way it was ignored by much of the press and Radio One. Even those who didn't get the power and fury of 'This Is Music' or 'A New Decade' couldn't help but respond to 'History'. Unfortunately, though, most mainstream music fans never got to hear it or even read about it. Richard couldn't help but compare the way his record was treated to those by other indie bands of the time. He regarded it as a masterpiece and he couldn't understand why the press and the public didn't seem to feel the same.

"*The Bends* and stuff like that was getting blown out of all proportion," he said to Darren Taylor. "Great record but Radiohead hadn't even come close to *A Northern Soul* yet. They're a fabulous band and they've got great songs but if you're looking for real rock 'n' roll, hip–hop psychedelic madness, which fuses all this stuff … *A Northern Soul* to me was like our *Revolver*."

In fact *The Bends*, too, was largely ignored when it was released.

The Verve and Radiohead were both seen as too dark to have wide appeal at a time when songs like Blur's 'Country House' and Oasis's 'Roll With It' were the dominant sound. *The Bends* only really took off through word-of-mouth and its ultimate inclusion in many 'End of Year' polls. There were many parallels between the two bands. Radiohead, too, found the touring treadmill difficult to stomach. They almost split up in 1995 but overcame their problems and, like The Verve, would release one of the biggest albums of 1997. After *A Northern Soul,* though, this kind of breakthrough for The Verve looked extremely unlikely.

During the dates they played over the summer, relationships in the band became increasingly strained. Part of the problem was just that Nick was so unhappy. Even after great gigs, he would still find something troubling him and The Verve's gigs had always walked a tightrope between brilliance and total collapse. When they played Glastonbury for the second time in 1995, they were once again hit by the Verve voodoo as his amp exploded, just as it had two years before. In reality it wasn't a massive problem, Richard just played the maracas until it was fixed and, years later, Glastonbury organiser Michael Eavis's daughter Emily Eavis would declare that their performance was one of her favourite Glastonbury memories. But to Nick it felt like nothing was going right.

1995's festival was one of the most successful for years. The sun shone for a change. Oasis were headlining and Pulp put in one of the great shows as last minute replacements for The Stone Roses. The Verve got good reviews but the band still weren't satisfied. That summer the antipathy between Richard and Nick began to escalate and, after they played T In The Park on August 5, Richard stunned them all.

Reactions to the gig had been mixed. Some fans and critics later said that they could see The Verve were on their last legs. There were reports that Richard looked unwell, stumbling around before punching Sobbo and hurling his cymbals across the stage. "The Verve are now dragging out the sublime 'Gravity Grave' to such ludicrous week-long extremes it could almost fill a Roger Dean-designed triple-LP bastard concept package on its own," said *NME*.

Elsewhere, however, some critics still thought things were going well. "The Verve hypnotise the audience with their laid-back but epic rock," said *The Observer.* It seemed like Richard, at least, didn't agree.

"We got on the bus afterwards," says John Best, "and Richard said 'that was the last Verve show, I'm leaving. I can't do this anymore.'"

The reaction was shocked silence.

"I don't know if anybody else knew that it was coming, but I didn't," says John.

"We've known each other for such a long time," Simon Jones told the Launch website, "that when Richard said he had to [break up the band], instead of everyone saying, 'Oh no, don't do it' and whatever, we accepted it. I don't think we were enjoying the music anymore."

"You can either carry on and be a business arrangement or a commercial arrangement," said Richard Ashcroft in a later TV interview, "and lie to yourself and lie to your family. Or you can say, well, sanity is more important than being in a band."

Even people close to the band weren't sure exactly what had happened. The fact that within two weeks Richard was once again working with Simon Jones and Pete Salisbury inevitably made many people think that the 'split' was little more than a way to push Nick McCabe out of The Verve.

"It felt like splitting up was just a way of not saying that Nick had left the band," says Phill Savidge. "If you say 'Nick's left the band' then the winner of the argument is Nick but if you say the band's split up then there are no winners."

Later on, Nick would take much of the responsibility for the split on his own shoulders. "I was being a miserable bastard, basically," he said when he was back in the band in 1997. "They got sick of my fucking sad face all the time. I just got paranoid about everything. So they sacked me."

Band members and friends have hinted since then that there was a lot more going on than anybody knew about. "That was completely insane that they split up at that point," says Brian Cannon. "It's not my remit to tell you why, or why I think that happened, that's very personal to the band members themselves."

"For me," says Miles Leonard, "what was difficult was seeing Richard always pulling Nick along or standing behind him and encouraging him that what they were doing was brilliant. From early on, Richard probably had the energy to do that. But you can only pull somebody along for so long. Towards the end they probably played one of the best gigs they'd ever played and Nick came off and said he didn't think it was any good and it was the straw that broke the camel's back."

For Nick's part, he often found that constant encouragement dispiriting. In 1994 American magazine *Hits* asked him what he liked most about Richard Ashcroft. "What I like about Richard is what I sometimes don't like about him," he replied, "his endless enthusiasm. I got up this morning and felt absolutely terrible and homesick. Richard said, 'Come on, get some life into you!' That can be a bit much really."

Although The Verve didn't use the familiar euphemism 'musical differences' to explain their split these, too, may have played their part. "Nick got into techno, for instance," says John Best, "and I don't think he wanted anything to do with the music they were making at the time. Nick's musical taste changed and he started twiddling with samplers and synths and stuff."

'History', the second single from *A Northern Soul*, was almost universally recognised as a highly fitting swansong for the band but there were a few dissenting voices. One paper, *The Strathclyde Telegraph*, misread the situation spectacularly. "Hands up those who like The Verve," they asked rhetorically. "What's that, about three, no maybe four or even five? To be honest, The Verve were the most overrated thing since Christianity. Both are based on men with long straggly hair and both will never come back."

Most commentators took the view that they were splitting up just as they seemed to be getting somewhere but even their death throes turned out to be much quieter than Richard would have liked. The music media, essentially, just shrugged and said goodbye. There was one final irony, though, in the cover art, which suddenly took on a whole new meaning. There were two versions. One featured them standing in front of an abandoned cinema with a sign on the front reading 'Life Is Not A Rehearsal'; the other, with eerie poignancy, read 'All Farewells Should Be Sudden'.

"That was the maddest cover of all," says Brian Cannon. "I got flown to New York to photograph it and I thought *Why the fuck are we doing this in New York?* It's obviously a very English song. *Where*

am I going to get a location here? We were walking down 42nd Street
– which is a real sleazy street – and I saw 'Life Is Not A Rehearsal'
on a theatre and we photographed them in front of that and it
worked. It was entirely accidental but it worked. It was a gift from
heaven. They're clearly a blessed band. But I didn't have the faintest
clue that they were splitting up at that point."

Richard had written 'History' about his break-up with Sarah but
it seemed almost prophetic. Indeed, Nick McCabe did once wonder
aloud if some of Richard's songs – particularly 'History' and 'The
Drugs Don't Work' were aimed at him.

Whether 'History' and 'The Drugs Don't Work' were odes to
Nick, only Richard knows but the release of 'History' as a single
provided a last act for The Verve that was strangely dignified
considering what had come before. It was also their biggest hit and,
for many, the first – and now final – indication that this band was
more than just a bunch of space cadets.

But almost as soon as Richard told them he was leaving, he
started to have second thoughts. Late that summer, he went on
holiday to Cornwall and, two days later, sitting in his hotel room, he
heard 'History' being played on Radio One. "I was more choked
than I've ever been in my life," he said later. "I was sure that if we'd
toured after 'History', we'd have taken off."

He was probably right, too. Fans everywhere were wondering
what had gone wrong. "I wasn't so much shocked as gutted," says
Michael Spencer Jones. It was more a case of, 'Oh no, the world's
been robbed of some great music. How did they let that happen?' I
was aware that there was this friction within the band but it seemed
to come out of the blue.

When I was doing the cover shoot for 'History', there was no real
indication that they were going to split up at that point. They didn't
seem to be arguing. I don't know what it was. I was aware that
certain things had happened with the band that had created some
friction. [But] they weren't really a band that argued. Maybe if
they'd been more vocal about it they'd have stayed together for
longer but they kept everything below the surface.

They'd done a lot of touring and I don't think they were getting
the recognition that they deserved. There was so much touring and
nothing was really breaking for them. But the ironic thing was when

they broke up the first time, they were on the verge of breaking America. I can remember thinking it was a crazy time to split up when they were on the cusp of making it big."

CHAPTER 8

A BAND APART

Although Nick was hit hardest by the split at first, spiralling into further depression, he probably benefited from it in the end. He went to see a doctor and then disappeared back up to Wigan to be with his daughter Ellie. "I thought, *Yeah, this could be my life now*," he told *The Face*. "Just sign on, relax, not worry."

Meanwhile, Richard was preoccupied by the thought that he might have just thrown away the dream he'd had since he was thirteen years old. Even worse he had already written great songs like 'The Drugs Don't Work' – but he had no band to play them with. The response he got to the new songs when he performed them at a solo support slot for Oasis at Madison Square Gardens helped convince him that he needed a band. "That was mad, really," he said. It just showed me that I'm not a solo artist. I felt so alone up there."

However, at least he was happier in other areas of his life than he had been after the drug-induced psychosis at the end of the *A Northern Soul* sessions. In 1995 he'd started seeing his old friend Jason Pierce's ex-girlfriend, Kate Radley. In April 1995, shortly before the first single off of *A Northern Soul* came out, he had been sadly bemoaning his single status in interviews. "I do need someone else to stabilise me," he told *Select* magazine. "Like the song says ['This Is Music'] 'I've been on the shelf too long.'"

However, he'd clearly fallen deeply in love because on July 11, 1995 Richard and Kate got married in Stroud, south-west England. Hut boss Dave Boyd once said that he thought Richard, "fell in love with her the day he met her." The relationship provided him with the love and support that he'd been looking for. And now he had somewhere settled to live for the first time in years!

"Richard seemed to be living in all these different places before that," says Phill Savidge. "He kept moving around. Then when he met Kate he moved in with her and I've got the feeling that that was the first time he'd really lived anywhere in the time I knew him. Before he was just existing."

This came across in the difference between songs he'd written before going out with Kate, such as 'The Drugs Don't Work' and songs he wrote afterwards like the much happier 'Lucky Man' and 'Sonnet'. For the first time there was a sense of contentment in his music.

"A lot of the problems when The Verve split up originally went back to Richard's problems in his personal life with his girlfriend," says Michael Spencer Jones. "[The third album] *Urban Hymns* is basically the songs he wrote when he split up with her, combined with the songs about meeting Kate. All that energy of the trauma of splitting up with somebody is put into the music. That's what makes it a great album. The songs that carry on from 'History' are set against the ones with a more optimistic note."

In 1996, Richard was slowly riding the roller-coaster back up to the top after the lows of the previous two years and he was determined to do whatever it took to become huge. He'd been spending more time with Oasis and he was intrigued by the way they operated. Apart from anything else, the lifestyle they had was beyond anything he could afford.

"Richard went to the Oasis Loch Lomond gig [in 1996] and he was hanging around with them the whole weekend and he could see the future for Verve!" claims Phill Savidge. "Without The Verve, Oasis wouldn't have happened," Michael Spencer Jones says. "They did all the groundwork and paved the way musically for Oasis. They educated an entire audience. It's very difficult to be an influential band but The Verve influenced a lot of bands, really. Somebody once commented that it's amazing that music came from four lads from Wigan."

But in 1995, even before they split up, the "four lads" were only together when they had to tour. Richard spent much of his time writing on his own. "Richard had lots of songs because he had a lot of time on his hands," says John Best. "He had a whole body of songs. The split happened in August and then in September he was in the studio and, lo and behold, Simon Jones and Pete Salisbury were in the studio …"

Although three quarters of The Verve were now back in the Real World studio in Bath with John Leckie, Richard was adamant that it wasn't The Verve without Nick McCabe. The sessions were intended to either be Richard Ashcroft's first solo album or else the new band would be given an entirely different name. It soon became apparent, though, that they were missing a lead guitarist.

Their first attempt at solving this problem was to bring Simon Tong in. Their old friend from Winstanley could play keyboards and complement Richard's own guitar. However, it soon became clear that they still needed to replace Nick. The sessions were highly successful, producing 32 demos including 'Sonnet' and a track whose working title was 'Stones Song' but John Leckie had to tell them that it wasn't going anywhere.

"We never got anything finished," he said. "Richard was looking for his Keith Richards. We also knew each other too well." Leckie also felt the gap left by McCabe. "Then in the spring we went with Owen Morris again," says John Best, "for what was supposed to be a week but it turned out to be two days because Owen said 'We can't do this because you don't have a guitarist!'"

So the band had all these great songs that would go on to form the nucleus of *Urban Hymns* but they couldn't quite make them work. "I said to the boys, 'What are we going to do? We need a guitarist,'" says John. "And they said, 'Yeah, but it's got to be an amazing guitarist!' And I'm like, 'Who are the best guitarists? It's John Squire, Bernard Butler, these sort of people.'"

Fortunately, by then, the critical acclaim that The Verve had received for *A Northern Soul* meant that they could afford to aim that high. They may not have sold the vast quantities of records of Oasis but both John Squire and Bernard Butler were no longer in the bands that had made them famous and the idea didn't seem unrealistic.

"I was with Richard at a party and John Squire was there," says John Best, "and I said: 'Look, that's John Squire over there. He's not in the Stone Roses any more. Why don't we ask him if he wants to be the guitarist in your band?' And he said 'I couldn't, I couldn't.' So I went over to him and said, 'I'm with Richard Ashcroft and I don't want to be presumptuous but would you ever consider playing guitar with him.' And he looks over at him and goes (shaking head)

'No, he does too many drugs!'

Then, through doing Suede, I knew Bernard Butler ... and they all went 'Great idea!' So I asked [Rough Trade boss] Geoff Travis ... and he said: 'I wouldn't have thought Bernard would be interested but I'll ask him.' So he asked him and, surprisingly, he said 'I would love to do it!' So I'm like, 'I've just created a super-group!'"

Ever since he left Suede during the recording of their second album *Dog Man Star* Bernard Butler had seemed to be looking for something to replace what he'd lost. He'd formed a successful partnership with David McAlmont but by the end of 1995 that, too, was on the rocks. He was very receptive to the idea of joining The Verve.

But this time it was Richard who wasn't convinced. He'd only ever worked that closely with his childhood friends and the idea of recording with a complete stranger, especially one with Bernard Butler's high profile, was extremely unnerving.

"Richard went, 'I dunno, man. I dunno'," says John. "I said 'Why don't you just try it? You might like it.' And a week went by and Bernard's ringing me going, 'What's happening? When can we meet? I want to do this.' So in the end I sent a car round. I sent a taxi for Richard to meet Bernard. 'Just fucking meet him!' So they met and got on really well and that day they went and recorded all afternoon. I've never heard what they did. It lasted about a week ... I actually think it's quite interesting that there is, somewhere, these recordings of Bernard Butler playing Verve songs."

"I said to him at the end of it, 'Look, you've got your own thing to do, I've got my own thing to do and there ain't space for it,'" Richard said to Q magazine. "Sometimes chemistry works and sometimes it doesn't, and in this case it didn't. But I left with only total respect for the geezer. He'd been in a band with people he didn't communicate with whatsoever and he was off on his own battles."

The problem may have been that Richard perhaps wanted something impossible – a great guitarist who would be happy to simply play without demanding creative control. "I was feeling a bit demoralised because we had all these great songs but both the producers who'd worked on our previous records were telling us we couldn't finish them because we didn't have a lead guitarist," says

John. "I was thinking 'What now?' I suppose in the absence of knowing how to find the right guitarist, I continued on the course of trying to find the right producer. So I had a long list of people but we couldn't agree on anyone."

Everybody was aware that The Verve had 'challenged' their previous producers John Leckie and Owen Morris in their mission to create the perfect record. They'd been lucky in that both of them had thrown themselves into the process willingly but they weren't confident that all big-name producers would be so congenial. They had to find the right person.

"I had this idea that, because Richard had this hippy, spiritual side to his personality, alongside the sort of Man Utd side, that he might get on well with Youth of Killing Joke," says John Best. "Youth's studio in Brixton was very Goa. It was post-acid house. That was the vibe I got from it. So I said to Richard: 'I think we should go and meet Youth and see how we get on with him.' So we went down to Butterfly in Brixton and we got on very well. He had loads of guitars and I think one of them was Eric Clapton's guitar. And Richard was like, 'Aaahh! Can I play it?' and he picked it up and played 'Lucky Man' and I'd never heard it before. I think he'd just written it."

Martin 'Youth' Glover had originally been the bassist in Killing Joke, a dark, post-punk band who'd been influential on Nirvana and many other bands, but more recently he'd made a name for himself as a producer for bands who ranged from the avant-guard to the completely mainstream. He was unsurprisingly impressed by 'Lucky Man' and in the middle of 1996, Richard, Pete and the two Simons went into Olympic Studios in West London, where the Rolling Stones and The Who had recorded many of their albums.

Once again they changed things in response to the mistakes made during previous sessions. Youth imposed a new discipline on their working methods. They would come into the studio at 10a.m. work solidly all day and then go home in the evening. He also encouraged Richard to shed his Stone Roses influences and head for a classic rock sound. More significantly he encouraged him not to give up on the 'Stones Song' demo that was soon given a new name – 'Bitter Sweet Symphony'. The old name, however, would come to seem painfully appropriate.

The Verve during an early Glastonbury performance.
Olly Hewitt/EMPICS Entertainment/PA Photos

Richard backstage at Lollapalooza with legendary
funk musician George Clinton, 1994.
Steve Double/Retna Pictures

Ashcroft with The Verve supporting Oasis at Earls Court, London, 1997.
Roger Sargent/Rex Features

The Verve in 1997: Nick McCabe, Peter Salisbury,
Simon Tong, Simon Jones and Richard Ashcroft,1997.
Roger Sargent/Rex Features

Ashcroft listens to a playback in the studio, 1998.
Chris Floyd/EMPICS Entertainment/PA Photo

Richard and family at *The Magic Roundabout* film premiere, London, 2005.
Richard Keith Wolff/Retna UK

Ashcroft warming up prior to an England vs Germany
Legends charity football match in May, 2006.
Justin Goff/UK Press/PA Photos

Ashcroft gets stuck into his solo set at the 2006 Isle of Wight Festival.
Simon Sarin/Retna UK

Richard and Kate at the 2006 British Grand Prix, Silverstone, UK.
Sutton/PA Photo

Richard headlining the *NME*/Radio One stage at T In The Park, July, 2006.
Duncan Bryceland / RetnaCelebs

Reunited and back on form, The Verve
play The Roundhouse, London 2007.
Dean Chalkley / Retna Pictures

Peter Salisbury and Richard Ashcroft, London, 2007
Dean Chalkley / Retna Pictures

Ashcroft sporting a new cropped, blonde hair-do during a
Verve gig at Nottingham Arena, 2007.
Dean Chalkley/Retna Pictures

'Bitter Sweet Symphony' was built around a loop of an orchestral version of The Rolling Stones' 'The Last Time' made by their manager Andrew Loog Oldham. Richard Ashcroft and Wayne Griggs had found it on an album called *The Rolling Stones Songbook* which they picked up in a second-hand record shop in Withington, Manchester. Richard said afterwards that he listened to it and thought, "I'm going to take this and turn it into one of the greatest pieces of pop-art the world has ever seen!"

The *Rolling Stones Songbook* was Andrew Loog Oldham's attempt to prove to the mainstream that the Stones were great songwriters by the somewhat ambitious means of having their biggest hits re-recorded in lounge music style. This was supposed to show that, underneath the rock 'n' roll mythology of the Stones (which he'd helped to create), was a songwriting partnership that could succeed in any genre.

The Verve had always liked using loops and samples but often they were so subtle that few people noticed. To begin with, though, Richard Ashcroft wasn't sure he'd be able to do anything with 'Stones Song'. Youth, however, was more enthusiastic.

Just before Christmas 2006, they started recording strings with Will Malone and Richard had an idea. They created two different arrangements for the song, based around the chord structure of 'The Last Time', and then chopped them up and looped them.

"I wanted something that opened up into a prairie-music kind of sound," he said to *Rolling Stone*, "a modern day Ennio Morricone kind of thing,"

The finished version of the song was far more than its source material. Essentially Richard did the same thing with it that he did with the tracks on *A Storm In Heaven* – almost unfurling the vocal in one long spiel over the top of an already established bed of music. He said later that the lyrics came out of his obsession with Arthur Miller's play *Death Of A Salesman*, which he'd studied at school, and particularly the central character Willie Lomax. Willie is the archetypal ordinary guy, struggling unsuccessfully to make something of himself. He's constantly chasing money but in the end he dies with nothing.

From these bleak roots, though, the song itself grows into something which sounds much more positive. They layered the vocal several times to give the effect of a heavenly chorus of Ashcrofts and then Wil Malone looped the strings to create a grand counterpoint to Richard's sermonising lyric. By that point it was clear that he'd become increasingly confident in his ability to actually say something through his songs.

"You've got to open up yourself," he said to *Melody Maker*. "And that's why lyrically, after five years, I've opened up on this new album. I've learned to take away the bullshit, get rid of the excess imagery. Sometimes you can hide behind words," he continued, "and I think I've got to go through a process of getting to the point where I don't need to hide any more. Why hide?"

While the rest of the world thought that The Verve were finished, Richard had quietly been writing some of the biggest songs of the Nineties and, in characteristic fashion, he knew it before anybody else. He even had an album title already.

"I remember Liam Gallagher at Knebworth shouting 'Richard Ashcroft get your shit together', in front of 250,000 people," he told Gary Crowley, "but fortunately I had *Urban Hymns* in the bag so I was feeling pretty cool!"

In retrospect Knebworth was the high water mark of Britpop. Two and a half million people applied for tickets and 375,000 people saw Oasis play over two nights. For every other band in Britain, it dramatically raised the bar. For a brief moment it was as though commercial success was not only cool, it could actually be seen as a real barometer of how good a band were. This might seem obvious but if you said to an 'indie' band in 1991 that quality could be measured by record sales or ticket sales, they would have been either amazed or appalled.

In 1996, Richard knew that, rightly or wrongly, millions of people thought that the reason Oasis sold more records than The Verve was because they were better than The Verve. He'd been particularly disappointed by their failure to make much of an impact outside of the UK and he started to wonder whether John Best was the right man to help him reach Knebworth status. To his great credit, John says that The Verve were the first band he'd ever managed and that, as a result, he did make mistakes.

"I think what put the rot in my relationship with Richard was that I was excitable about music in general so I was doing a lot of things," he says. "I had three different companies and I was juggling things. I think he thought: 'I should be number one. Why aren't I number one all the time?' Because sometimes I'd say 'I can't do this, I've got to do something with Brett or Jarvis'".

He had also inadvertently introduced Richard to his next management team when he took him to see Youth, whose own management was Big Life, headed by music biz legend Jazz Summers. "He said that he liked him because he was, 'a maverick like me.'"

Jazz Summers could also tell a hit when he heard one. From that first moment at Youth's studio in Brixton, he could hear the massive potential in the new tunes. "As soon as I heard the songs for the new album, I told Richard, 'With my experience and your talent, we could go all the way!'" Jazz told the *LA Times*. "I remember he looked across the table at me and asked, 'What's all the way?' I said, 'You can be the biggest band in the world.'"

Jazz Summers had been a manager since the early Seventies, originally working with folkie Richard Digance, but by now he had a strong reputation for being able to break unlikely British artists in the States. As co-manager of Wham, he'd come up with the idea of making them the first Western band to play in China. On the back of that they received huge amounts of publicity in America and became absolutely massive. Later on he helped Lisa Stansfield to sell millions of record internationally and he successfully promoted Soul II Soul in the USA when most Americans had little idea that there were any black musicians in the UK.

This was the main reason Richard wanted to work with Jazz's Big Life organisation. While Savage and Best were highly successful with credible Britpop bands like Suede and Pulp, Big Life offered Richard a chance to leave behind the 'indie' sensibility that he'd had in the past. He wanted the kind of success that Wham! had achieved.

As John Best said, a lot of people had their eyes on the prize in the mid-Nineties. The success of Oasis had changed the pop landscape. They had proved that bands with guitars and indie hair could make a mint. By 1996, Britpop may have run out of ideas but few people realised that at the time and, besides, The Verve were different. Right from the start they'd assimilated whatever was going on around them while giving it their own twist. They had elements of retro-worshipping Britpop but they weren't afraid to use new technology. They retained an outsider edginess but with Oasis's desire to make songs that the whole world could sing. It also helped that Richard Ashcroft had such natural star quality and, just as importantly, a willingness to flaunt it and use it to get ahead. Unlike Oasis, who had a songwriter, Noel Gallagher and a star, Liam Gallagher, Richard Ashcroft in 1996 did both jobs himself. That was to prove a problem ultimately but to begin with it meant he was able to do whatever it took to realise his vision.

While Oasis were in the studio making the album that would herald their decline, *Be Here Now*, Richard was about to surpass them for the first time since 1993's tour. Not by accident, either. He'd always believed that it was only a matter of time till the world woke up to his genius but, in 1995, he'd realised that if he wanted that to happen he had to write songs that could reach a whole new audience. There were many different steps along the road to megastardom – the right management, the right record label, the right PR, the right look. The biggest step, however, was always the right tunes and he'd got them by the bucketful.

For once his timing was spot on. They were about to catch the last wave of a movement, Britpop, with songs that were far stronger than the ones most of their contemporaries were putting out. Britpop had come to mean retro bands like Cast, The Seahorses and Kula Shaker. More innovative acts such as Blur and Pulp had retreated from the poppiness of their earlier incarnations and were busy making much more melancholic records like 'Beetlebum' and *This Is Hardcore*.

Rock music, on the whole, was becoming more conservative. Britain was starting to be flooded with Oasis clones. Few people guessed it at the time but within a couple of years Britpop, as a genre, would be dead and British music would be in the doldrums. "I don't think we really missed out on much being away," Richard commented later. "The last 18 months haven't been the most colourful fucking period in English music have they?"

But, as the first demos for what would be *Urban Hymns* started coming together, Richard was still worried. He wondered if his songs were missing something. The new sense of direction that Youth had given them had helped, but their structured sessions sometimes felt stifling compared with the freewheeling, late night jams that they were used to. The first track they'd tried to record, 'Space And Time', had been particularly frustrating. The first version was too fast and so they tried again the next day but it was too slow. This went on right up until Christmas but somehow they just couldn't get it right.

"The thing with The Verve is they are a feel band," says John Best. "They will play a song eight times and record every one and it's not like they're minutely different – they're completely different. They'll do one that's really fast and then they'll do one that's half the pace."

Simon Clarke of The Kick Horns, who rejoined them briefly at Olympic, said he noticed a distinct difference in the atmosphere. "My memory of that as an experience is not nearly so strong as the *Storm In Heaven* sessions," he says. "It felt like when we went to Olympic that we were working more like session musicians. We came in, did our thing and then went away. I felt slightly less connection with the band."

"I remember at the time thinking it was pretty much Richard's show," says saxophonist Tim Sanders. "Youth was producing but I don't think any of what we did was used. We were doing a similar thing to what we were doing on *A Storm In Heaven* but I just didn't really see the point. I just thought, *What are we doing here?* We were just fattening things out. I didn't really think it was necessary. But then as a session musician you don't really have a sense of the big picture. That's the job of the band and the producer."

Despite the quality of the new songs, both of The Kick Horns had a sense that something wasn't quite right with the Olympic Sessions. "Often in those situations, either a band isn't getting on with a producer, or they're not getting on with each other, or the material isn't yet formed, so they're having a stab at it and they decide to redo it later," says Tim. "So many different factors come into play. You're not going to be aware of that on a one-off session. You can't know what's going on really."

Richard knew what was going on. He was telling himself that what he was doing had nothing to do with The Verve. He missed the almost magical feel that recording sessions used to have at their best when Nick McCabe was in the band. Despite his misgivings, he eventually decided that the guitarist was the missing part of the puzzle of *Urban Hymns*.

"When you get the inner voice calling you," he said to *NME*, "you can deny it for a while but when it starts eating at your insides you have to answer it, you have to heed its advice, because that's your instinct and your instinct is the truth. In anything in life, a relationship or whatever, don't deny your instinct."

Once he'd made the decision, he didn't wait for long but there was a problem – Nick seemed impossible to contact. He called him at his flat in Wigan but there was never an answer. He then tried his mum but he wasn't there either. Finally he managed to track the guitarist down to a friend's flat. In typically dramatic fashion, he reportedly told the guitarist that if he didn't rejoin The Verve, then he'd quit music forever!

Only the night before, Nick had had a dream about getting his old job back at the surveyor's office. It wasn't a nightmare, either. It was a happy dream of freedom and security from all the stress and madness that he'd endured in The Verve. Wisely or unwisely, he chose to ignore his own instincts. Richard was still a master at getting people on his side. He would do whatever it took. "He had to eat shit," Nick told *The Face* later. "I told him, 'I ought to tell you to fuck off but I'm glad to hear from you!'"

"The Verve without Nick isn't The Verve basically," said Brian Cannon. "Because Nick is The Verve. The Verve is Peter Salisbury, Simon Jones, Nicholas McCabe and Richard Ashcroft. That's The Verve. They're the sum of their parts and minus any of them they were fucked, I thought."

CHAPTER 9

URBAN HYMNS

"On *Urban Hymns* 80% of the songs were written by me," Richard Ashcroft told the *Wigan Observer* after the band's second break-up. "It was going to be my solo album. It was a month away from being my first solo record."

It's hard to judge now how different Richard's story would have turned out had he not put the call in to Nick. Songs like 'Bitter Sweet Symphony' and 'The Drugs Don't Work' would have been hits whatever name they were released under and, although Nick had some input on both of them, it wasn't as significant as on previous material. Despite this, he knew exactly why Richard wanted him back in the band. Nick was there to take these new songs and dirty them up a bit, place them back in the gritty lineage of *A Storm In Heaven* and *A Northern Soul*.

Later on, Richard perhaps seemed to have wished that *Urban Hymns* had been his first solo record. "It would have been great to stamp those tunes firmly as mine," he said to Gary Crowley, "so people didn't try to make up some cock and bull story that it was only these key characters that could create a song like 'The Drugs Don't Work' or 'Lucky Man'."

At the time, the band were delighted to have Nick back in the studio. Many of the songs that they'd already worked on ended up being completely re-recorded so Nick could add his own touches. One of the first things he worked on was 'Bitter Sweet Symphony'. He created the strange, swirling guitar sounds that come in just before Richard's vocals. It was a classic example of what he was there to do – adding just the tiniest touch of grit to Richard's gorgeous, shimmering pop song. Contrary to popular belief, Richard had no desire to make a middle-of-the-road album.

On 'Velvet Morning', for example, he deliberately dirtied things up himself by finding an old megaphone and gaffer-taping it to the microphone. Engineer Chris Potter was slightly dubious but it gave the song a faraway, detached quality that stops it from being mawkish. The title of the song was a homage to Lee Hazlewood who wrote the duet 'Some Velvet Morning' for Nancy Sinatra. Richard wanted the same kind of raw, gruff effect that Lee frequently used as a counterpoint to Nancy's sweeter tones. It still needed something extra, however, and Simon Tong was despatched to borrow a pedal steel guitar from the artist recording upstairs – Eric Clapton! That was one early sign of the different world they were starting to live in.

For a while it was the ideal situation. Richard and Youth had set the original direction of the record, a more classical sound, moving away from their psychedelic leanings. Then when Nick came in, he had a new confidence in his importance to the band. He said in one interview that he "felt like a 16-year-old again … I've benefited most out of this, really," he said, "cos I've got a sense of whatever goes wrong doesn't really matter, 'cos I fell to the bottom and it wasn't so bad."

He also publicly took the blame for the split but Richard admitted that they'd all made mistakes. "He might have had problems," he said to *NME*, "we all had problems. But I didn't have empathy. Didn't have life experience enough to be able to cushion and deal with it. I have now."

Gradually, Youth had taken more of a backseat and let Chris Potter became more involved then, shortly after Christmas 1996, Youth departed from the project entirely. Chris then began collaborating with the band on the production. Like Owen Morris, he was originally an engineer rather than a producer. He, too, didn't have many high profile production credits before working with The Verve. That suited Richard fine because he didn't want anybody telling him how his record should sound. Nick McCabe got on well with Chris too and the sessions became ever more productive. To begin with, his role was supposed to be merely recording some of the guitars but Richard decided that, with Nick back in the band, they needed more songs.

Before that could happen, though, The Verve were confused to discover that some of the first recordings from their Olympic Studio sessions were circulating on the internet. Things were changing as rapidly in the music industry as they were in the band. Only two years before it was relatively rare for fans to swap audio files online. Now, in American college circles especially, it was commonplace.

The label also had to counter many of the rumours flying around that were entirely inaccurate. One Dutch magazine reported that Noel Gallagher had said Richard was now the head of a new band called Sensation and their new songs were "very, very, very good". Then when *Select* magazine wrote a joke article alleging that he'd formed a Rolling Stones cover band called Rockery this was also regurgitated straight-faced by the rumour-mill.

In February 1997, they went back into the studio and re-recorded two lost tracks from the *A Northern Soul* sessions – 'Rolling People' and 'Come On'. They were both songs that they'd somehow failed to capture last time but the new versions were much more powerful. That inspired the whole band to feel that they were about to recapture the energy of 1994.

In May 1997, things accelerated further. They went into Olympic Studios again for just ten days and came out with five new songs: 'Weeping Willow', 'Catching The Butterfly', 'Stamped', 'Three Steps' and 'The Longest Day'. It was an extraordinary session. They just jammed without really knowing where they were going while Richard sang whatever came into his head over the top and Nick tore strange sounds out of his guitar.

'Stamped', 'Three Steps' and 'The Longest Day' all ended up as B-sides but the other two songs were good enough to put on the album. 'Catching The Butterfly' was originally about half an hour long and even in its final edit it still sprawls out over a magnificent six minutes. 'Weeping Willow' was almost as long. They initially recorded it on a day when Nick was away at a wedding but, when he came back, he blazed some tremendous psychedelic, effects-twisted guitar over the top of what they'd done. Producer Chris Potter was astounded by what he came up with.

"There's what I call a talking guitar after the second verse," Chris told the-verve.info fansite. "Nick's guitar seems to say 'oh, yeah' or something. I've no idea how he did it."

It wasn't quite the chaos of *A Northern Soul* but it was still a shock for Chris Potter to see how they worked. They still liked to record at ridiculously high volumes and, because the sessions had dragged on longer than they'd initially expected, there was pressure to get everything done. By the time he came to mix the record, Chris would be there from the middle of the morning till gone four the next morning. As with all of The Verve's producers, though, he found himself quickly drawn into their way of doing things. Once again this meant walking along a tightrope with them between their psychedelic side and their pop side. Just before the Olympic Studio sessions started, he'd said he was going to give up smoking. Not surprisingly that resolution was put on the backburner until the last track had been mixed – almost nine months later.

The last song they recorded was 'Neon Wilderness'. They'd almost finished mixing the rest of the record when Nick started working on a guitar loop. The rest of the band added bass and drums before Richard contributed another brilliantly ad-libbed vocal over the top. Having started the session at six p.m. in the evening they finally had the song finished to their satisfaction at five a.m in the morning.

It must have been an incredible feeling. *Urban Hymns* is a bizarrely misunderstood album. Some purist early Verve fans often choose to see it as the moment Richard Ashcroft sold out and went for mainstream pop songs but, in reality, two thirds of the record is every bit as out-there as anything on *A Storm In Heaven* and *A Northern Soul*. At the same time it takes a certain churlishness to ignore the brilliance of the album's pop singles. Despite this, some fans evidently wanted them to carry on making the space rock of their debut.

"What a stupid idea," Roger Morton says, "they'd already made the cosmic rock records with those kind of songs on them. What were they supposed to do? Carry on doing that forever? That's ridiculous!"

Urban Hymns had tunes that anybody with even a slight interest in popular music could relate to but it was, simultaneously, The Verve's 'mature' album. This is made very clear by the opening strings of 'Bitter Sweet Symphony' which say that, if previous Verve albums had worn jeans and a t-shirt, this one was dressed up like James Bond.

The second track, 'Sonnet', is another example of Richard's new found love of songs with, as he put it, a beginning, a middle and an end. It takes things down a notch in intensity from 'Bitter Sweet Symphony' but its laidback approach betrays a new confidence. He didn't feel like he needed to push things as much as he had in the past. It's a song that's figuratively leaning against the wall watching the world go by. This is very clearly not the collaborative Verve of the past. If 'Sonnet' had ended up on any debut Richard Ashcroft solo record, it's unlikely that it would have sounded any different. It's one of several songs on the record which are vehicles for expressing the different emotions he'd been through in the last few years. On these tunes he was determined to express his feelings even more than he had on *A Northern Soul*.

But, despite this new spirit of soul-baring, *Urban Hymns* wasn't a pseudo-Richard Ashcroft solo record in all but name. 'Rolling People' brings the old Verve hurtling back in a mighty rush. It starts with some gale noises, as though it's being recorded in a desolate wilderness somewhere. Then the groove, when it comes in, is classic Verve, with Pete's drums at their most thunderous and the riff making classic rock shapes above. It's another example of The Verve functioning as one. There's the old intensity and freedom of their jamming, with Richard ranting over the top, almost sounding as if he's trying to sing the riff like a kid playing air-guitar, but there's also a great chorus.

It's the high before the beautiful low of 'The Drugs Don't Work'. Like 'Yesterday', this song should have lost its power by now through repetition. But there's a reason why it was the first of The Verve's singles to go to number one. While it's not a tune to lose yourself in like the best tracks on *A Storm In Heaven*, it has that unique ability to connect on an emotional level, on first listen, which is the mark of a truly great pop song.

The balance between songs like that and next track, 'Catching The Butterfly', is what makes *Urban Hymns* such an unusual, often incredible, album. 'Catching The Butterfly' starts by coming on like one of The Beatles' experimentations with Eastern music but in the background there's what sounds like a riff being played down a concrete tunnel. It's a weird mixture of bucolic psychedelia and something much more brutal and industrial. Lyrically it goes back to one of The Verve's original themes: lucid dreaming – the ability to visualise something special and then chase after it.

The next track, 'Neon Wilderness', is a kind of cousin to 'Brainstorm Interlude' on *A Northern Soul*. It's the only song on the album to be credited to McCabe/The Verve and it functions as a kind of palate cleanser halfway through the album. There's no real hook or chorus, just what sounds like a continuous outro, two and a half minutes of fading out, Richard's vocal uncharacteristically low in the mix, babbling away as Nick creates a wash of ambient guitar in the background.

The next song, 'Space And Time', may have been the first track that Chris Potter worked on but it would ultimately be one of the last tracks they finished. They kept working on it, chopping and changing and, as a result perhaps, it doesn't quite know what it wants to be. It has elements of a classic Ashcroft ballad alternating with sudden splurges of rock. Neither aspect work as well as they might. Towards the end it's not completely clear where the song is going and they seem to have run out of ideas.

But 'Weeping Willow' picks things up again with a yearning vocal from Richard that slowly turns into a mantra. Over several minutes, Nick gets his guitar to talk to Richard – literally according to Chris Potter – but also figuratively. It was one of those moments where the whole band came together. The next track, 'Lucky Man', was pure Richard Ashcroft. It was well-placed so late in the album, breaking up the space rock with something simpler and cleaner sounding. It seems almost like a duet between Richard and the string section, rather than a traditional Verve song. The lead guitar was played by Simon Tong, rather than Nick, and the difference is noticeable. Simon's style is much cleaner and brighter.

The next track, 'One Day', is another one of Richard's quiet ballads, more like the kind of work on his later solo records, rather than a big emotional statement like 'The Drugs Don't Work'. Instead of strings filling up all the space, Richard's voice is multi-tracked so he's duetting with himself, with the vocals crossing over.

Then 'This Time' sees Richard defiantly promising, not for the first time, that one day he would fly. It's a great song – one of the tracks that the success of *Urban Hymns*' singles probably overshadowed. According to Chris Potter, it was originally called 'Discordant' – maybe because of the way the different elements – the drums and Richard's background piano assault – clatter against each other. The overall effect is similar in its hypnotic sound to certain songs on *A Storm In Heaven*.

'Velvet Morning', too, is a classic Ashcroft pop song in not particularly subtle disguise. The use of the megaphone and the pedal steel guitar give it a warmth and a slightly weathered feel, avoiding the blandness that he'd later slip into with some songs during his solo career.

There's no danger of that with the last song on *Urban Hymns*, 'Come On'. It's the only track on the record that has the aggression of *A Northern Soul*. Like 'Rolling People', you could guess without being told that it came from the same sessions. It has the same slightly unhinged quality with Richard ranting and howling "fuck you!" as the guitars are let off their leash like rottweilers. Apart from the vocal, the whole song was recorded in one day, live, and that gives it a ferocious energy that's a great ending to such a varied album. For millions of the people who bought *Urban Hymns* on the strength of 'Bitter Sweet Symphony', it was probably the most aggressive song they'd have in their record collection.

With The Verve's third album they didn't play it safe. It wasn't an album of twelve 'Sonnets'. It was yet another, largely successful, attempt to somehow synthesise the two sides of The Verve. They had an unusual problem. They were brilliant at two very different disciplines that often seemed mutually contradictory. They could do classic pop songs like 'The Drugs Don't Work', which formed the next link in a seamless chain of rock history stretching back to Elvis and earlier. But they also had the desire to make rock music which sounded as fresh and modern as Nineties dance. It was a conundrum that they didn't entirely solve on *Urban Hymns*. On most of the songs, the classic and the modern are side-by-side rather than integrated, but they did prove that they could create amazing music in both directions.

"A lot of albums tend to be on one kind of level where as *Urban Hymns* is very melodic in places, very heavy in places, very soft in places, very hard in other places," Michael Spencer Jones says. "Musically it's got everything. When you stick it on, it's like listening to a compilation album. It's got all these moods going on. When you listen to it you're not putting yourself into one particular mood, you're going on a bit of a rollercoaster."

The last piece of music on the record was a hidden track – some radio noise, distorted muttering, gentle chords and the odd sound of a baby crying in a deeply eerie fashion. It was called 'Deep Freeze'. After their second break-up, it would be ten years before relations within The Verve would start to thaw enough that they could record again.

Before that, though, with 'Bitter Sweet Symphony', Richard had a single that would give him everything he wanted – and then take it all away again.

CHAPTER 10

STONES SONG

Youth had suggested 'Bitter Sweet Symphony' as a potential first single right from the start but Chris Potter and others had been dubious. However, by the time it was completed, nobody had any doubts. The only problem was getting clearance for the sample from the Andrew Loog Oldham song. Permission was certainly not a given.

"That loop, just for the record, is very little," Chris Potter told the-verve.info later. "It's a basic chord progression and a couple of bongos, it's not the string riff." The loop they took was a relatively small part of 'The Last Time' but, with much more luxuriant strings draped over it, it was the central part of 'Bitter Sweet Symphony'. Anyone listening to the Loog Oldham tune now without knowing about the controversy would think it was a weird, instrumental cover of 'Bitter Sweet Symphony'. Richard Ashcroft's use of the sample was reminiscent of hip-hop sampling in that he took the best bit of a song and made it much better.

Initially they were optimistic that they'd be able to get clearance for the song. They heard that Jagger and Richards liked their track but, unfortunately, the copyright was owned by the rather less enthusiastic manager Allen Klein and his ABKCO organisation.

"I don't care if everyone else in the world allows it, I don't agree with sampling as a matter of principle and certainly not on a Stones song," he was reported to have said, by Robert Hillburn of the *LA Times*. That could easily have been that but The Verve decided the track was too good to abandon and so Jazz Summers attempted to persuade Allen Klein's company ABKCO to change their minds. His strongest argument was that 'Bitter Sweet Symphony' could end up being a huge hit, making them a great deal of money. They weren't interested.

Jazz then contacted Ken Berry, the president of EMI who now owned Virgin and thus put out both The Verve and The Rolling Stones' albums. Ken Berry loved the track, too, and went to Allen Klein's office to play him the song. To everyone's surprise he liked it and, for the first time ever, allowed a sample to be used.

Everything seemed to be fine but they hadn't bargained for quite how big a hit 'Bitter Sweet Symphony' would become. It went straight into the UK charts at number two, only held off the top spot by the release of Puff Daddy's tribute to the Notorious BIG *I'll Be Missing You* (itself centred around a sample of the 1983 Police track, 'Every Breath You Take').

Then it became public knowledge that The Verve would not receive any split on the record sales. "At the moment I'm too pissed off to even fucking talk about that situation," Richard said to *NME*. "Basically … we took a bit of string and a bit of bongo and built … the … fucking symphony … around it. With an orchestra, with various tracks of guitars, fucking vocals, feedback, bells, the lot and made this inspiring piece of music and got it fucking taken away for legal reasons."

At a time, 1997, when the most successful 'indie' bands had revelled in sounding like they came from the Sixties and the Seventies, The Verve actually sounded very modern despite their use of the orchestral sample. Once again Richard's talent didn't just lie in his vocal skills but also in the way he got the best out of his collaborators. On 'Bitter Sweet Symphony', that was effectively Mick Jagger, Keith Richards, Andrew Loog Oldham and string maestro Wil Malone. "The good thing about me," he once said, "is that I'm kind of limited as a musician, but I have a giant imagination."

From the day it was finished, everybody involved knew that it was potentially a huge hit but they also knew that a large chunk of money would be heading in the direction of Allen Klein's organisation. This was from a song that went straight into the UK charts at number two becoming by far their biggest hit. And there was more trauma to come.

The Verve had never allowed any of their music to be used on adverts, despite receiving lucrative offers but several agencies expressed an interest in using 'Bitter Sweet Symphony'. As usual, they said a firm no but, although they had control over their recording, they didn't have control over the song itself. ABKCO had control of the publishing and in theory could hire musicians to make another recording of the song if The Verve wouldn't authorise their version.

Jazz Summers pointed out to the band that they didn't have much choice. They were faced with the possibility of their song being used to promote General Motors, Nike and many others. In the end, they agreed to let just Nike use the track in the hope that that would prevent anybody else from using it. They also donated the fee to the British Red Cross Landmines Appeal and to a London homeless project Youth 2000.

One side-effect was that the Nike commercial ensured their track got far more exposure across America than it ever could have done from radio play alone. Before it aired, *Urban Hymns* had been out for a month and reached a chart peak of 63. Afterwards it climbed into the top 30.

Ironically, because 'Bitter Sweet Symphony' was longer than the standard three and a half minute pop track, many American radio stations simply ignored it. Somebody even called Richard to say that he needed to cut the track down. He told Corey duBrowa of American magazine *Magnet* that he was warned, "If you don't edit 'Bitter Sweet Symphony' yourself, someone's gonna do it at the radio station, they're gonna take a chunk of your music out and it won't get picked up as a 'play' on the central computer."

In the end, Richard Ashcroft had to accept that 'Bitter Sweet Symphony' wasn't a song he could control with the same equanimity that he accepted the loss of all of his possessions when he didn't pay the rent. With barbed wit he described it as, "the best song Jagger and Richards have written in 20 years."

He did have some kind of moral victory when Andrew Loog Oldham sent them a letter which they reprinted in the artwork of *Urban Hymns*. He said that he loved the track and that "the Stones were probably too old to remember where they nicked that particular riff from themselves". In this he was being slightly unfair to Jagger and Richards. The Rolling Stones version of 'The Last Time' was heavily inspired by 'This May Be The Last Time', a traditional gospel song recorded in 1955 by The Staples Singers.

Because it was traditional and long since out of copyright, however, The Stones were not obliged to pay a penny.

"It had a strong Staple Singers influence in that it came out of an old gospel song that we revamped and reworked," Keith Richards said. "And I didn't actually realise until after we'd written it because we'd been listening to this Staple Singers album for ten months or so. You don't go out of your way to lift songs, but what you play is eventually the product of what you've heard before."

The Verve, in contrast, had always prided themselves on the fact that, unlike a lot of Britpop bands including Oasis, they didn't write songs by apparently stitching together bits of the past. "I can honestly say we never sat down and said, 'We want to be a cross between the Beatles and whatever, with a bit of this and a bit of that,'" Richard told *Rolling Stone*. "We've never done covers. We only played what came out."

Despite the problems, 'Bitter Sweet Symphony' did its job. It made millions of people aware of The Verve for the first time and it helped *Urban Hymns* sell 750,000 copies in its first week. This was despite the fact that the first Verve live date for almost two years had to be cancelled at the last minute. They were supposed to play at the Sheffield Leadmill on June 14, 1997 but, just a few days before, the stress of the *Urban Hymns* sessions caught up with Richard. He said afterwards that the lymph glands in his neck had swollen up "to the size of footballs". In rehearsals, every time he tried to sing any of the rockier songs, he was in huge pain.

"I never got to the point where I was truly up for it, to be honest," he said to the *NME*. "For one I was in the middle of finishing the record, so you've got to look after your energy levels, and two, I was very ill. Everyone else apart from me was gagging for it... Whatever it takes wasn't there. And what we do is just too big to go out there at anything less than 100%."

But 'Bitter Sweet Symphony' didn't need to be toured to become a hit. It was helped on its way by a video which became one of the most watched, imitated and parodied of the Nineties. It showed Richard walking down a street in Hoxton, east London, staring straight at the camera, looking gaunt and intense, bumping into people and brushing them away without even noticing. It was actually itself a kind of homage to an earlier video for Massive

Attack's classic *Unfinished Sympathy*, which featured vocalist Shara Nelson walking down a street in Los Angeles, ignoring everything and everybody that she walked past. But, where Shara seems merely absorbed in her own thoughts, there's more belligerence and aggression to Richard. It perfectly captured his single-mindedness, not to mention his ability to brush aside people who got in his way or who couldn't keep up.

"It looked real because I actually was pissed off when I was doing it," he told Siobhan Grogan of *Glamour* magazine. In the end he partly regretted the fact that the image of him walking down the street with a defiant stare came to define him.

"The 'Bitter Sweet Symphony' video was almost like creating a monster," he said. From then on, whenever he walked towards anyone down a narrow street he realised that they were having flashbacks to that video. Van drivers would pass him and shout: "Ere, mate! The video's finished!"

"I was walking away from a lot of things that I perhaps treasured," he told Dave DiMartino of the Launch website. "I like privacy. I like being a voyeur on the street, rather than the one that's being watched. But I danced with the devil and I have to take the flak for that."

CHAPTER 11

STARDOM

In the mid-Nineties, celebrity culture exploded like never before in the UK. Being 'famous' wasn't the same as it had been when Richard first dreamed of being a rock star as a thirteen-year-old. Suddenly there was obsessive interest, not just in the music that he made, but in everything else he did.

"I went from being on the dole to suddenly selling millions of albums," he told Siobhan Grogan. "Designers would offer me anything I wanted just to sit on the front row of a fashion show. The next offer would be even more ridiculous. I realised I had to sidestep it all or I'd always be stuck in that vacuum of late Nineties celebrity culture."

When he went on holiday for a brief break, he realised that his celebrity had spread beyond the shores of the UK, too. On a visit to Rome, dozens of people followed him and Kate down the street, snapping him with their cameras. At one point they were even tailed in their taxi by two girls on scooters.

"I saw the Vatican for fifteen minutes," he complained to *Rolling Stone*. "I was saying to these people, 'You come halfway around the world to see this place and you're looking at me! Get a fuckin' life! Come on, you're in the Vatican!'"

When he got home from Rome it was to find his and Kate's face on the front of the country's biggest daily newspaper. Although by then they'd been married for about two years, the tabloids had recently discovered their relationship and broadcast it to the world in classic tabloid-speak as "Heart-throb rock idol Richard Ashcroft of The Verve is having a wild affair with rock babe Kate Radley."

This kind of thing touched much more of a nerve than any other coverage he received. When they hit the gossip columns again after the Phoenix Festival, Richard was fuming. "I love Kate, that's it, that's all I've got to say about it," he said to *Vox*. "If anyone tries to demean anyone in the situation, in print, they'll be getting a baseball bat over the head from me, simple as that."

Not long afterwards Richard's ex-girlfriend Sarah was interviewed by a tabloid under the headline, "Why I Dumped Rock's Hottest Property!" For the first time, the mainstream was interested in Richard and his fans no longer came exclusively from the narrow demographic of cool indie kids. Suddenly all kinds of people were asking for his autograph or stopping him in the street.

"I used to be able to tell by the cut of somebody's jeans whether they would stop me," he said to Gary Crowley. "Then suddenly a track seeps into different parts of society and you can't judge who it'll be."

This sounds like a complaint but it wasn't supposed to be. Richard had always wanted his music to reach out beyond the narrow world of the music press and student radio. He expected and desired global recognition. But, having been a huge fan of the Stone Roses and other bands who had crumbled under the pressure of success, Richard was well aware of the pitfalls that were to come.

"Look at bands that get to this position and see how many get torn apart from the demands put upon them," he said. Yet with disarming openness, he was always honest about the fact that he relished his success and proving so many people wrong.

"There's part of me wants to pull up outside me school in Wigan, where they said I was the cancer of the class, in a Rolls Royce Silver Phantom and say 'Hello, I want to play some songs to your class'," he told *Q*'s Michael Odell. "And there's part of me that wants to hide out in a Cornish fishing village and never come out for 50 years."

Immediately after The Verve's first break-up, when he suddenly realised that, once again, he'd run out of money, he wasn't averse to using his new fame to tide him over. In 1996 he earned several thousand pounds modelling for fashion designer Mossimo. It wasn't something he felt comfortable doing, however.

"I was absolutely [broke] and desperately needed some money," he told *Alternative Press*. "It was a case of down and out – you've gotta do something when you're down and out. Everyone has sold to the fucking devil at one point in their life."

Similarly none of the videos that they made for *Urban Hymns* seemed to feature somebody who wanted to be a recluse. They all lingered lovingly on Richard to the exclusion of almost anything else. Most of them barely included the rest of the band, except fleetingly in the background. Richard was acutely aware of the power of a video to sell his music and of the fact that there was a lot more to selling records than simply writing good songs.

"It's not up to the bands or the artists, success is about radio programmers and MTV controllers," he told Darren Taylor. "This day and age, you can tour a band to death and build up a certain following but albums explode because they come with a video and radio decides to support a band that they never supported before."

He thought that part of the success of *Urban Hymns* came from the fact that radio stations, particularly Radio One, belatedly realised that they should have paid more attention to 'History' and *A Northern Soul*.

"They've got a big guilt trip about not getting behind *A Northern Soul*," he said, "and so has 90% of the British press. They just gave it a little footnote in the albums of the month. People missed it."

With 'Bitter Sweet Symphony', then, The Verve had become 'the Richard Ashcroft Show' in many of their new fans', eyes but it was to be the second single off the album, 'The Drugs Don't Work', which would prove that they didn't need the Rolling Stones or Andrew Loog Oldham to have a massive hit.

"There's a new track I've just written," Richard Ashcroft told *Select* magazine in 1995. "It goes 'the drugs don't work, they just make me worse …' That's how I'm feeling at the moment. They make me worse, man. But I still take 'em. Out of boredom and frustration you turn to something else to escape."

That's a pretty simple summary of what the song was about. In the final version, though, the 'makes me worse' was changed to 'makes you worse' causing all kinds of speculation about it. One particularly poignant interpretation was that it was about the death of his father. Brian Cannon isn't alone in being positive that that's the case.

"It's about Richard's father not being able to respond to the drugs that were being prescribed to him," he says. "It's about his father's death rather than anything else. If you asked Richard, I'm sure that's what he'd tell you."

There's not much concrete evidence to suggest that this is true but it is one perfectly reasonable theory about the song's meaning. Richard didn't seem to be singing it in a self-pitying way, however. His vocal had a rawness that came from the fact that he captured it live on the first take with Simon Tong, Simon Jones and Pete Salisbury. Chris Potter later said it was one of the best vocal takes he'd ever heard.

At times Richard, predictably, got very involved again. He asked that the popular Saturday morning music programme, *The Chart Show*, run the video without any of their trademark captions. The show, inevitably, refused but this didn't dent the band or the song's popularity. Whether they liked it or not, they were now writing pop music in the truest sense.

It became the band's first number one single in the UK – topping the charts the week Princess Diana died when suddenly the airwaves were full of mournful music. Unfortunately its success might have once again made Nick feel alienated from the band. Even though his slide guitar had played a small part in the song's success, he'd never particularly loved it. It was a huge departure from the messy, raw, psychedelic sound that they'd worked so hard on only a few years before. To the vast majority of the public, The Verve were now the band who made clean pop songs like 'Bitter Sweet Symphony' and 'The Drugs Don't Work'. When he played on those recordings, Nick can't have fully realised that they would so completely overshadow everything else he had ever done in his musical career. He wasn't alone in feeling that the 'real' Verve were under threat.

"It's my least favourite Verve record if I'm being honest about it," says Brian Cannon. "And to be honest, it's my least favourite sleeve. I'd rather not talk about that sleeve. It had nothing to do with me that. You can tell, man. That had nothing to do with me."

The sleeve for 'The Drugs Don't Work' is simply the title and the band's name picked out in yellow and white against a black background. The stripped down style, once again, fitted the music but it wasn't the kind of music that Nick liked too much. It was hard to argue, though. The enormous success of the record saw to that.

One of the many things that made 'The Drugs Don't Work' such a hit was the way that it could 'have its cake and eat it'. It was raw and edgy, being about drugs, man, and yet nobody in the mainstream could complain about it because it was so unambiguously anti-drugs. It was also an all-purpose lament that anybody could relate to, whether they'd lost a loved one, suffered a broken relationship or were just dealing with the effects of a comedown or a hangover.

"I see 'The Drugs Don't Work' as a love song," Richard told *NME*. "Not about drugs not working but about being that far down and you realise that they're not getting you to where they used to. Don't get me wrong though," he continued. "I'm not doing a Nancy Reagan and saying 'don't do it.' Whatever gets you through the night that's fine by me. I'm just saying that we've been there, y'know, and I think a lot of other people in our generation have been too. It's not some fuckin' *Grange Hill* version of life."

Although Nick McCabe might not have liked the song, his slide guitar also adds just enough edge to the record to stop it turning into something overly saccharine and middle of the road. It isn't just the acoustic guitar ballad that it's been painted. Wil Malone's strings are once again superbly sympathetic to Richard's melody, allowing it to breathe. The vocals, too, go way beyond singer-songwriter clichés as Richard allows himself to lose it towards the end, scatting manically in almost evangelical, gospel style over the fade-out.

But it was its campfire appeal that took it to the top of the charts. Even more than with 'Bitter Sweet Symphony' it was one of those cross-generational pop songs that appeals to children and much older people as well as the core audience of teenagers and twentysomethings. There may have been a handful of people who, like Brian Cannon, missed the more expansive, rock 'n' roll Verve of *A Storm In Heaven*, but there were thousands of others who discovered them for the first time.

It helped that, as they'd started to write more commercially viable songs, their record label suddenly started to push them harder, too. Legendary American-born publicist Scott Piering, who sadly died in 2000 and had an industry award named after him, was behind the radio push. The KLF famously said of Scott in their book *The Manual (How To Have a Number One The Easy Way)* that, without him, "this book would have to be retitled How To Get To Number 47 — With A Certain Amount of Difficulty."

But it was the deceptive simplicity of the song that made it so successful. Like Oasis's 'Wonderwall' 'The Drugs Don't Work' was one of those rare songs that enters the busker's songbook — always a sign that a song has hit a major nerve. Richard would later talk about hearing of a bar band in Kenya playing it. Its ubiquity almost seemed to frighten him a little. He worried about the fact that they'd become so successful with such a dark, sombre track. Slightly touchingly, he also worried about the fact that young children were being exposed to a song about misery and despair.

"It worried me," he said to *News Of The World*, "because I never wanted to appeal to young kids. Our music isn't innocent or superficial and I don't like to think of all those kids listening to some of our darker tracks." He didn't mention that during his own childhood he'd had to deal with rather worse things than a song. There were signs that commercial success was having the same negative effect on the band as failure.

The photo shoot for *Urban Hymns* wasn't the happy, exciting experience that previous shoots had been. Although one Verve fan has declared that, if you analyse the skyline, the way Richard's hat and the trees line up spells out the word 'Love', it doesn't seem like there's anything quite that clever going on. It was intended to be their simplest sleeve yet. Richard's attitude was "just listen to the fucking record."

"That was a bit fraught," says Brian. "That's the biggest selling Verve sleeve but I'm not happy with that. The band sat in the fucking park! It didn't work for me, that. It'd all gone by that point. I just think that you could see the end of the band there. The joy had gone, shall we say. I just wasn't into it. Having said all that, the record is amazing. The record is fucking incredible. But because of the in-fighting in the band, I don't know what it was, I wasn't let in. It wasn't like the old days."

"We went to Richmond Park to do the photoshoot," remembers Michael Spencer Jones, "and there was another photographer involved who was going to do some shots at the same time, which I found fairly awkward. I think he was setting up his equipment and they were sat down waiting to be photographed by him and

I happened to notice that they'd relaxed so I thought 'I'll have that' so I got them just at that moment. They weren't aware that they were being photographed, they were just looking at some deer in the background. It created a competitive edge but the irony of that is that the cover of *Urban Hymns* is a photograph of them waiting to be photographed. Without the other photographer being involved, I wouldn't have had the luxury of photographing them like that so all's well that ends well!"

For all the awkwardness creeping into The Verve's internal relationships and the relationships with the people around them, Richard relished the fact that at last he was getting to where he'd always said he'd be. "I don't see popularity as something to be afraid of," he told Robert Hilburn of the *LA Times*. "Most of the bands that I loved were popular, from The Beatles to the Stone Roses. It is the most exciting thing in the world to know that there is all this excitement over your record or your next concert."

The week 'The Drugs Don't Work' came out, they were headlining the *Melody Maker* tent at Reading Festival. The fact that Metallica and Marilyn Manson were on the main stage might have been a sign of the direction the music scene was going, with metal about to come back to the fore, but they still pulled a massive crowd. "Imagine watching the main stage tonight when you could be in here," Richard announced as he walked on stage.

"They've talked a magnificent fight for years, while not quite fulfilling all the propaganda and potential. Now, though everything is right," one reviewer said. Then, in September, they supported Oasis during three nights of the biggest indoor gigs ever at Earl's Court in London. Richard was ecstatic that, thanks to their recent success, he could almost compete on the same level as the Gallaghers. "Talk about a fuckin' celebration," he said to *Vox*. "Dream material. They've done it before, but I still think us being with them there makes it even better. And every fucker in that room's gonna know who we are as well, it's not 200 people at the front, bored."

A week later, on September 29, 1997, *Urban Hymns* was released. Such was the excitement by then that it became the fifth fastest selling album ever. It went platinum in under two weeks and would become a fixture near the top of the album charts for months.

Ultimately it would go on to sell seven million copies as the band toured and promoted it in a way that they never had for *A Northern Soul*. For many people who'd supported them from the beginning it was a vindication.

"It was incredibly gratifying to see a band that you'd believed in for so long finally achieve the success they deserved," says Miles Leonard. "They'd always written songs that were very creative and exciting, just not necessarily performed as pop songs, and I always had faith in them to deliver at some point. The first album ultimately wasn't a success in a commercial sense but the band developed through those albums and suddenly it all culminated in *Urban Hymns*.

I only saw it as an extension of what they were doing previously. It was what they always led you to believe they were capable of doing. They were true to themselves. They're an honest band, they always have been and it was a natural progression. The great songwriting talent of Richard came through but it was the sum of the four parts of that band, or five parts with Simon Tong."

And according to Michael Spencer Jones, all five parts knew exactly what they'd created. "There was still a good vibe," he says. "Throughout everything the focus was on the music and the music was creating the vibe. When I first heard *Urban Hymns*, I went into the studio and it just sounded absolutely amazing. There was a great atmosphere being generated by the music alone. They were aware that they were sitting on this great body of work."

In a TV interview at the time, Richard was still saying the same things that he'd always said, "With luck on our side we could become the biggest band in the world," he announced. "And the biggest band in the world with a bit of integrity." But this time it seemed like it might actually be true.

For once, commercial success and critical acclaim came hand in hand. The reviews were largely ecstatic. "Its greatness is in its humanity," wrote *Mojo*, "and in the sense that, from fear, failure and insecurity, it's possible to scale heights in a way which not only sets the standard for the rest of the year, but the decade, too." And *NME* described it as "the musical signature of the year for anyone not so out of love with music that they're satisfied with Elton John's bleeding heart." The response in America was just as excited. In

Rolling Stone, John Wiederhorn wrote, "*Urban Hymns* is a breathtaking venture, an ambitious balance of stargazing and worldly pathos."

At the end of 1997, tickets went on sale for their world tour and, in Europe, they sold out in under two hours. This time Richard was determined that they wouldn't have to postpone. Before the start of the tour, at the beginning of 1998, he took himself off on a two week holiday to Majorca where he slept and did his best to eat fruit and vegetables for a change. It must have worked because for once they made it to the airport without anybody breaking any bones or falling ill! The gigs themselves were much bigger than any of their previous tours, with giant slogans beamed against the wall behind them. Some of them were obvious Ashcroftisms like: 'Think that you are somebody and you'll be somebody'. Others were more cutting: 'A psychotic is just a guy who's found out what's going on'; and 'Virtue is not photogenic'.

What made their success even better for Richard was that he felt that they'd done it without compromising their principles. "It wasn't success that was important," he said to Darren Taylor. "It felt like it would be a fucking moral victory if we were successful. The good guys were winning. We were like gangsters that made people feel good. We said no to things most people would say yes to. We did different things. We lost control of 'Bitter Sweet Symphony' in terms of it being used in advertising and that was like a blip. We wanted to do it without having to do any of that shit."

Inevitably this attitude would, at times, cost them. When 'The Drugs Don't Work' was released in America, they were invited on presenter David Letterman's popular *Late Show*. This was supposed to be a huge honour with guests fighting to get on. But, when the band got there, they were asked to cut the song down to approximately three minutes by starting it halfway through. "They don't fucking understand," Richard said to Darren Taylor. "That two-bit actor or actress you were interviewing will be dead and buried in three years. This is one of the best songs of the Nineties that we're prepared to stand in your studio and perform and you'll have it on tape forever; on your tape with your name on it."

They refused to cut the song and so the credits began rolling as they were halfway through. "What's frustrating," said Richard, "is that when you look back on Ed Sullivan's archives of people that played on his show [in the Sixties], admittedly Elvis and the Stones and The Doors all had to make changes to their performances but he gathered some of the greatest acts of all-time that he could put on a reel. There's no feeling of importance anymore. There's no feeling of looking forward to the future."

But, despite this, The Verve were now very much flavour of the month in the music industry. At January's Brit Awards, they had five nominations: 'Best Album', 'Best Band', 'Best Video' and 'Best Single' as well as 'Best Producer'.

In the album stakes, they were up against Radiohead's landmark *OK Computer,* a record which, within a couple of years, would frequently feature at or near the top of lists of the best albums of all-time. It was no less than Richard expected or thought they deserved but, typically, the idea of sitting down to accept the acclaim of a group of people who'd given them nothing for so many years didn't appeal, either. Instead of attending the ceremony at London's Docklands Arena, they elected to perform at a Homelessness benefit at Brixton Academy instead.

They weren't the first or the only band to effect an air of cynicism towards the industry's backslapping fest but The Verve genuinely didn't appear to care all that much. "Having a cynical, sardonic attitude about stuff like that," Richard said, "is difficult 'cos you come across as an arrogant cunt, but I'm not interested in all that. Awards and all that – who cares?"

At the awards themselves, a similar air of cynicism prevailed. There was the traditional moment of controversy when left-wing agit-pop veterans Chumbawamba threw a bucket of water over the Deputy Prime Minister John Prescott, but otherwise it was most notable for the absence of several of the winners. Nevertheless, when the industry had to choose between the bleak, awkward, brilliance of Radiohead and The Verve's somewhat more accessible sounds, there was only one winner. They eventually won, not just 'Best Album' but also 'Best Band' and, along with Youth and Chris Potter, 'Best Producer'. The highlight for The Verve was being presented with the three awards they won by George Best who joined them on-stage at Brixton Academy before they performed their new single 'Lucky Man'.

'Lucky Man' was Richard's attempt at writing a song with the simple power of 'The Drugs Don't Work' but without the dark, macabre side. It's fringed with some of Nick McCabe's guitar effects but most of the lead was played by Simon Tong. And, once again, most of the space in the song that's not taken up by Richard's voice is filled by a vast orchestra. Although the strings are fairly subtle, the song is as as much a collaboration between Richard Ashcroft and Wil Malone as it is a Verve song.

This comes across very clearly in the video. They're in a vast, plush Nineties apartment overlooking the water. While Richard walks around singing and playing on the guitar the rest of them sit there looking immensely bored.

This might just be because none of the others felt as comfortable in the limelight as he did but it also made the point that it was his song. Just as with the first singles from *A Northern Soul*, the lyrics were very personal to him, too, describing how he felt about his new relationship with Katc. It starts off relatively low-key but by the end of the song his early description of being happy, more or less, changes into something much more ecstatic – a love that "won't die."

The next single 'Sonnet' was similar – an almost cautious description of either the birth or the death of a relationship set to swelling strings and acoustic guitar. As John Best said, The Verve were "taciturn Northern boys" and so Richard never exactly gushed in his love songs. The acoustic guitar melody is very restrained, too. Part of the song's charm is in the way it holds back. It's the strings, even more subtle than in 'Lucky Man', that carry the emotional impact without overdoing it.

Released as a limited edition in the UK, with four other tracks, it wasn't eligible for the charts but it was all over the radio and made them bigger than ever. The Verve's commercial peak came shortly afterwards with their massive show in the grounds of Haigh Hall near Wigan on May 24 1998. Upwards of 40,000 people poured into the 250 acre estate, including the 61-year old Mayor of Wigan and Nick McCabe's young daughter, sitting on her grandfather's shoulders.

For Richard Ashcroft, it was further proof of the power of positive thinking. He told Michael Odell that it was his stepfather who'd long wanted the band to play there. "Doug visualised the gig at Haigh Hall five years before it happened," he claimed. "He said 'I can smell the hot dog stands!' I'm not saying it's magic, it's the power of the mind."

Few of The Verve's long-term fans can have shared his belief that they would ever play to a crowd this size. In 1991, 'indie' bands didn't have that kind of pulling power. At Haigh Hall, however, the atmosphere was rabid and celebratory. This wasn't necessarily good news for the first support act John Martyn. The Verve were huge fans of the legendary Scottish blues singer but his spacey mix of folk and jazz was largely ignored by a partisan crowd.

The next support, Beck, had the same problem. At that point, he'd been a fairly constant presence on British radio with songs like 'Loser' but as he was playing his new hit, 'Devil's Haircut', a gang of people without tickets were kicking down the perimeter fence as the police struggled to regain control. "Wigan's football hooligans turned up with scaffolding poles," says Brian Cannon. "It was out of order actually because they attacked the security and they all got in. That was a fucking free-for-all!"

Beck eventually won fans over with sheer stage presence and energy but Haigh Hall wasn't quite the laidback festival that Richard had envisaged. Everybody there saw it as The Verve's triumphant homecoming, a complete vindication of the wild claims that they'd made at Winstanley College.

When they finally bounded on stage, Richard Ashcroft bellowed what had, by now, become his catchphrase – 'Come on!' Before a 15-minute version of the song of the same name, he captured what many people, not just the band, were thinking. "We've been saving it all up for this moment. right here, right now! Eight fucking years! Come On!" It was also their opportunity to reclaim 'Bitter Sweet Symphony' for themselves. "This song has been stolen," Richard announced before hand. "This is a song for the people. This is a modern day blues song."

"That was the most astonishing gig of all-time," says Brian Cannon. "There's no doubt about that. I was a massive Happy Mondays fan in the late Eighties but Haigh Hall, May 24, 1998, my 32nd birthday, was the best gig I've ever seen in my entire life. Not only because of the music but because of the crowd's reaction. It was fucking beyond belief. It was absolutely astonishing, man. I just went buckwild that day."

"It was top, coming from a town that'd given you fuck all, standing there saying, 'I did it!'" Richard said later. These were the moments he'd dreamed about when they first formed the band. When he later spoke to writer Darren Taylor, he compared the feelings he had before going on stage to taking a bungee jump. "It's that balance of the personality that leads idiots like me to end up in front of 40,000 people because beforehand you don't know if you're a Forrest Gump or a Jim Morrison."

It was an incredible day, not least because almost everybody the band had been to school with, their whole families and everybody they'd grown up with, was there. It was also the last time Nick McCabe would play with the band for nine years.

CHAPTER 12

McCABE vs ASHCROFT

The power struggle between singers and guitarists is part of the mythology of rock 'n' roll. Many of music's most significant names come in those pairs – Morrissey and Marr; Jagger and Richards; Townshend and Daltrey. The idea is that they act as a foil for each other, providing quality control and creating something that's more than the sum of its parts. If they argue, that's just more fuel for the fire. Their respective solo efforts, compared with what they have come up with together, generally reinforces the strength of their co-dependence.

Richard Ashcroft and Nick McCabe's relationship wasn't quite like that. Maybe if it had been, The Verve would have managed to stay together longer. They may have literally fought each other in the end, but for much of the time they just bottled things up. They didn't butt heads and create something out of the tension. They were either going the same way creating the ground-breaking music on the first half of *A Northern Soul*, or they were seemingly totally at odds with each other.

"When it's working it's amazing," Nick said, "but when it's not it's horrible." Nick's talent was deep but sometimes he found himself seemingly part of "Richard's band" along with Si and Pete, even though his playing style wasn't suited to simply standing in the shadow of Richard's vocals.

The whole of The Verve would often be frustrated by the fact that Nick didn't always seem to realise how talented he was. "Tell him he's fantastic," Simon Jones once asked a guitar journalist. "I think he's the greatest guitarist around and he won't have it. Tell him! He's amazing!" Nick would create incredible sounds and then ponder about the fact that he hadn't – in his mind – been able to do better. Despite this, he had no interest at all in being a virtuoso. "I think guitar players who strive for technical excellence have lost the plot really," he once said. He was just interested in what sounded good, rather than what showed off his talents as the clichéd guitar hero.

Where Keith Richards would give as good as he got when confronted with the ego of his songwriting partner, Nick would withdraw into himself, silently storing away his frustrations. "We had a joke in the band about me being the kitty litter tray. Any shit that happened to anybody I absorbed it," he said.

And there was a lot of shit going. This book has already touched on the drugs situation. On a more prosaic note, the bad food and lack of sleep of the rock 'n' roll life wasn't conducive to good mental health, either. Plus, he was constantly being told by Richard that what he was doing was incredible and yet, when they released the records, for the first five years, hardly anybody bought them. Then when they finally got the success that they deserved, he couldn't claim as much of the credit because some of the songs were already written before he arrived (eventually eight out of 13 are credited to Ashcroft).

Still, there was a reason why Richard kept asking him back. When they played live, the rhythm section of Si and Pete gave the vocalist the solid base that he needed to strike out from but it was the sounds coming from Nick's guitar that spurred him on. It was a unique partnership and one that Richard, significantly, never attempted to replicate with anybody else. He never worked with anybody remotely in Nick McCabe's mould. His week working with Bernard Butler was the closest he ever got. He knew that anybody who stepped into Nick's shoes would face unfair comparisons.

Ashcroft and McCabe has never become a brand name like Jagger and Richards because the songs where they met as equals, 'This Is Music' or, 'A New Decade', say, never became household names. But many Verve fans would say those songs were among their best. Those were the songs where Nick's ferocious independence, originality and love of noise gelled perfectly with Richard's mastery of arrangements and melody. This meeting of minds was witnessed time after time when they played live and it was one of the small tragedies of The Verve's recorded career up until 1997 that it wasn't always heard on record.

However, after The Verve became successful, not everybody could see the point of Nick's sonic odysseys. In a live review in *The Observer*, Barbara Ellen railed against what she saw as the over-complication of what could simply be a great pop band. "While the rest of The Verve seem determined to resurrect the bad old days of shoe-gazing, Ashcroft bounds across the stage like a self-igniting firework," she said.

But when he'd launched his solo career, Richard Ashcroft told Michael Odell that, when they broke up for the second time, he had no problem with Nick. "We had more in common at the end of the band than with any of the others," he said. "He's one of the most talented musicians I'll ever work with. An incredible artist and a beautiful person. Nick is the last person in that band I've got bad vibes with."

Nevertheless, it was Nick who had the biggest qualms about stepping back on to the tour/record/tour treadmill. It can't have helped that their biggest songs were now ones he'd had relatively little to do with. After Haigh Hall, the band were booked to play V98 and other festivals and then a lengthy US tour. Nick was initially happy to pay the festivals, which were very lucrative, but another long, gruelling tour of America didn't appeal. He knew that most of the fans would be unlikely to know anything off of *A Northern Soul*, still less *A Storm In Heaven*.

Eventually it was announced that, although Nick hadn't left the band, he wouldn't be joining them on tour for the dates. Tim Vigon, their then-PR man, tried to put as good a spin on it as he could. "Nick was never comfortable with the touring situation," he said. "He is a man of great principle. He just looked at the American dates and said 'I can't and won't do these.' Being trapped in a van just isn't on his agenda at the moment." None of them were exactly looking forward to getting back on the road. "It's been non-stop for months," Richard complained to Robert Hilburn of the *LA Times* at the Brit Awards, "and now we're supposed to go back to America for some more shows. It's just insane."

The one bright light was the recruitment of accomplished pedal steel guitarist BJ Cole. He was in his early fifties but he was regarded as one of the most innovative and original musicians around. He'd worked on the previous Spiritualized album and an impressed Kate

Radley recommended him to Richard. As a founding member of early Seventies country band Cochise, he had taken traditional country styles and given them a psychedelic, hippyish flavour. This was exactly what Richard was looking for. He knew that a traditional lead guitarist, playing 'licks' or riffs in the conventional sense, just wouldn't work.

A pedal steel is very different to a normal guitar. It's played horizontally and uses a metal slide to hold the strings down, rather than the fingers on a conventional guitar. This creates the keening, melancholic sound that's often heard in country music but very rarely in rock. At that point, The Verve had only ever used it on 'Velvet Morning'.

Richard wanted somebody who could provide something unique and different but who would be happy to fit in with The Verve's style. This summed up BJ Cole perfectly. Although Cochise never made much commercial impact, he had gone on to be a celebrated session musician throughout the Seventies and Eighties working with John Cale, Scott Walker and Elton John among others.

In a way, he was Richard's perfect playing partner – highly gifted and yet happy to remain in the background. He was capable of bringing just as much technical virtuosity to the table as Nick McCabe but without inviting direct comparisons.

"Richard rang me up and asked me to come and rehearse with him," BJ Cole told the author for this book. "I was very intrigued, being a pedal steel guitar player, even though I have played with rock 'n' roll bands quite regularly, working with a band like The Verve, with their profile, was pretty impressive and piqued my curiosity. It was quite an unusual thing to have a pedal steel player in a band like The Verve.

By bringing in somebody like a pedal steel guitarist they obviously weren't trying to replace Nick McCabe. I think by not doing the obvious thing and bringing in another guitar player perhaps they were thinking that there wasn't going to be anybody who could step into the big shoes that Nick McCabe had in the band. They wanted to do something that wasn't comparable."

At that time nobody wanted the band to split up. They'd even gone into rehearsal studios and started writing songs for the planned follow-up to *Urban Hymns*. Richard had dreams of writing new symphonies to prove, once again, that he didn't need the Rolling Stones or Andrew Loog Oldham. Although they may have initially been reluctant to go out on tour again, everybody was aware that, with 'Bitter Sweet Symphony' and 'The Drugs Don't Work' still slowly permeating into the public consciousness, they had a great chance to break America.

In retrospect, it might have seemed like they were falling apart but that's not the way BJ Cole, who'd had no experience of their previous conflicts, saw it.

"There was no suggestion that they were on their last legs as a band," he says. "The budget and the general push behind the band was all guns blazing, basically. It was one of my tastes of the rock 'n' roll lifestyle. It was fantastic! Expense accounts, limousines, and being taken out to dinner; just lots of money around and being feted."

When they got to America, they spent about a week in Chicago rehearsing furiously, trying to fit BJ's unique style into The Verve sound. "They had a strong identity," he says. "Not only was Richard a strong character but Pete was very strong and solid. I got on very well with Simon. I fitted right in. For Richard, bringing in a pedal steel guitar was obviously an experiment but they were aware that I could cut it musically and in a rock 'n' roll context, which was unusual for a pedal steel. On that level I think it worked very well.

Richard was very good. He let me be myself and find my place in the band as myself. Playing with Richard and The Verve reminded me of the dynamic I had with that Cochise band which I did a long time in the past. I was playing really loud, I was using a lot of effects, I was using a lot of distortion, like a rock 'n' roll guitar player would. Basically a pedal steel is an electric guitar, the dynamics are the same. You can treat it the same way as a lead guitar in that context."

In America, where many fans weren't aware of the historic importance of Nick McCabe to the band, they received a mostly positive reception, too. The *Michigan Daily's* Brian Cohen enthused: "The name Nick McCabe rang only the most muted bells, leaving instead the deafening sounds of a triumphant band determined to let the music speak for itself."

To outsiders there was an air of walking wounded among the band, especially when a few shows were cancelled or downsized.

After 'Lucky Man', they told the record label that they didn't want to release any more singles off the album, preferring to play live, but touring only widened the cracks that were once again starting to appear.

Later, Richard said that some of the performances on their last tour of America hadn't been up to their usual standards. He thought that the uncertainty about their future was affecting them all. "You know, when you're in doubt about the future and you're in doubt about how solid this thing is that you're laying your life and your soul on the line for, you will probably retract into yourself a little bit and think, *No, there's only so much I can give to something that everyone doesn't believe in*," he said to Jay Babcock of *Mean Magazine*.

It wasn't like previous tours. Because of their break-ups and falling-outs, it's easy to forget how close the band used to be. Outsiders were often amazed at how close knit they were and how much they loved being on the road.

"I went to North America with them," remembers Brian Cannon, "and it was absolutely outrageous, absolutely belting. The thing about The Verve was, unlike most other bands, they were *super* close. They loved each other and it was very much an intersociety, that band."

When they got back from America, the last show of the summer was on August 29, 1998 at Slane Castle in Dublin and it should have been the culmination of an incredible couple of years. For BJ Cole it was: "It was tremendous," he says. "When we came back from the States and played Slane Castle it was one of the high points of my career. Maybe the rest of the band were blasé by that point but I certainly wasn't. The thing about coming off stage at the end of the Slane Castle gig and being ushered up the back lane under cover of a firework display in a motorcade with a Garda escort was not lost on me, really."

But the rest of them were having darker thoughts.

"I think I knew that night that that was the last gig The Verve was ever going to play," Richard said to Darren Taylor. "Whether everyone was clear on that I don't know."

Simon Jones certainly had some idea that it might be the end of the road. John Squire was backstage at Slane and there were even reports later that Simon Jones started talking to him there and then about forming a new band.

"I think there was discussion after Slane of 'what are we going to do next?'" BJ Cole says, "but it wasn't 'Are we going to continue or aren't we going to continue?' In my experience it was just all very positive. Slane was obviously a very positive experience. There was a very big sense of event in that gig. But I think that's inherent in the place that it happened. Slane Castle is a really memorable place to do a performance."

Richard agrees with BJ Cole that Slane was one of the high points of their career. "It was an incredible gig," he told Darren Taylor. "A lot of things have been written, quite lazy journalism, that the last tour was really bad," he said. "It was a very stressful fucking thing for me. I nearly had a nervous breakdown on the last tour of America before we came back to Slane Castle. But the actual gigs, because of that, because there was so much mad energy going around, and because it probably was the last tour, they were fucking unbelievable.

They were amazing gigs actually. But after Slane it was a relief when we finished for me. I just wanted to get home after it. Get home, close the fucking door and re-evaluate and think about it and sort the situation out."

Whether or not fans liked the gigs probably depended on which version of The Verve they liked – "Captain Rock and his bunch of space cadets" or the new version writing songs that the whole world could sing. "The last tour without Nick, oh my God, it was awful," website host and fan Ajay Sharma says. "It was all *Urban Hymns* apart from a couple of songs from the other two albums. That's not good. I hated it."

Immediately after Slane Castle, rumours appeared on fansites suggesting that they were going to officially announce the end of the band within weeks. In reality, nobody was sure what was happening. The Verve were in a weird limbo with everybody waiting to see what would happen next.

Richard had already made one tentative step outside of the band. Before the success of *Urban Hymns* he got a call from James Lavelle, the boss of celebrated dance label Mo Wax. In 1996, Mo Wax had released the hugely acclaimed *Endtroducing* album by electronic artist DJ Shadow and, off the back of that, Lavelle put together a project called UNKLE featuring DJ Shadow's characteristic trippy, hip-hop sound alongside several guest vocalists.

Among other things, it showed an impressive gift for talent spotting. It included Thom Yorke, immediately before Radiohead became massive with *OK Computer*, Badly Drawn Boy a long time before his debut album was released and Richard Ashcroft before anyone had heard *Urban Hymns*.

DJ Shadow used to play The Verve's 'History' in his DJ sets alongside the latest West Coast hip-hop tracks and that was something Richard found hugely flattering. It was his dream for the kind of music that he made to escape any boundaries that were put around it. He wanted his records to be alongside Al Green and the best R&B and hip-hop, rather than just other British indie or rock bands.

In the end the record, which would be called *Psyence Fiction*, wasn't as good as everybody had hoped. It soon became symbolic of the over-used "trip-hop sound". Part of the problem was that, initially, UNKLE was pretty much the coolest thing in the world and, perhaps, the hype overwhelmed them. When it finally came out, a lot of reviews seemed partly concerned with punishing Lavelle for his hubris and his attempt to portray A&R as a kind of artform.

Nevertheless, many reviewers agreed that Richard's song 'Lonely Soul' was a major highlight. His voice sounded more tormented and darker than anything on The Verve's records and it worked beautifully over the muffled drum 'n' bass beats and stark strings. The arrangement suited him. His voice had room to breathe, sounding simultaneously powerful and haunted. When he sings about dying there are echoes of 'The Drugs Don't Work' but there's also a sliver of light in the way that the song embraces death, almost as a kind of freedom, not something to be afraid of.

As so often it was a one-take vocal. He listened to the music on the way to the studio in his car and did it straight with no lyric in front of him. It was an exciting taste of what life without The Verve could be like – working with the world's most talented musicians without having to worry about egos. In interviews after the record came out, he speculated about whether that might be the direction he'd take in the future. Nick McCabe might have found that a little ironic. The guitarist had always been the one who was into electronic music. Richard was torn between doing something cool and credible and his continuing desire to get his music across to as many people as possible.

It took him a long time to decide what he would do next. "I had varying thoughts," he said to Darren Taylor. "Thoughts of, *At the end of the day I've sold six million albums, maybe it's time to go and buy a place and live.* Just fucking live! Not deal with the rest of it."

It wasn't until the following April that The Verve were finally put out of their misery when they released a statement calling it a day. "I would like to thank the fans for their loyal support and their phenomenal response to *Urban Hymns*," Richard announced. "I feel more positive now a decision has been made – being in limbo isn't good for the soul."

Simon Jones left things slightly more open. "The remainder of the band – myself, Nick McCabe, Simon Tong – are continuing to work on our own projects, while Pete Salisbury is currently working on Richard's new album," he said. "The rest of the band might even work with each other in the future. If this happens, it won't be as The Verve."

CHAPTER 13

POST-MORTEM

"When I was growing up, I thought the only thing you needed to do was make a great record and everything would take care of itself in music," Richard Ashcroft said later to the *LA Times*. "But what I thought was the finish line is just the starting point. There's a reason they call this the music business."

It's a popular response from bands when they break up – to partly blame it on shadowy industry figures – but there may be some truth in it here. Certainly The Verve, collectively, didn't have the constitution for the kind of lengthy tours and two-year schedules that the world's biggest bands were signed up for.

But the real problems in The Verve were internal. Their history is sometimes seen, slightly simplistically, as a battle between the visions of Nick McCabe and Simon Jones on one side and Richard Ashcroft on the other with the easier going Pete Salisbury in the middle. On *A Storm In Heaven*, Nick's guitar dominates and the powerful, stormy, jam-session vibe that he and Simon Jones loves won out.

Then on *A Northern Soul*, Richard Ashcroft was starting to discover a new confidence in his songwriting talents, pulling the band in a completely different direction on certain tracks. By *Urban Hymns*, with Nick McCabe out of the picture for the first few months, his vision was dragging them out of the sonic swamp towards the sunny uplands of commercial respectability.

There's some truth in this but in reality Richard remained somewhat in awe of Nick's guitar talents even when they weren't getting on. And whatever Simon and Nick said later about preferring darker, heavier music to songs like 'Sonnet' they must have respected his talent, too, or at least his ability to write songs that sold in the millions.

Still, The Verve were very different to other great bands of the Nineties. If you listen to Nirvana or Radiohead albums you don't get the impression that they are about to fall apart in the same way that you do with The Verve, who sometimes seem to be on the verge of self-destructing even within a song. The more cohesive tracks often come across as Richard Ashcroft solo records with little touches of The Verve here and there.

Paradoxically the seven million sales of *Urban Hymns* made Richard feel he might have been wrong to have turned it into a Verve record. It gave him a confidence boost and made him feel that, after all, he didn't need a band to hide behind.

"Imagine being the guy that's written an album on his own, bottles it near the end, feels like there's unfinished business, rings Nick McCabe up who adds some guitars, puts it out as The Verve and the same problems arise again," he said to Dorian Lynskey in an interview with *The Big Issue* magazine. "Imagine being that mug. I've now got to rewrite history. Everyone thinks those songs are associated with a bunch of people that I'm not with now."

Nevertheless in interviews after The Verve split for the second time, he was generally careful not to denigrate his old bandmates. It was Nick McCabe, who'd rarely even been quoted in the media, who really let fly. Not long after the band announced that they were splitting up in 1999, he started emailing Ajay Sharma's fansite; this ultimately led to Ajay travelling to England to interview the guitarist and, when the interview was finally published in 2002, it proved incredibly impassioned and controversial. Some of the things Nick was quoted as saying were pretty inflammatory and seemed to utterly destroy the notion that The Verve would ever get back together.

The first time The Verve broke up they all seemed to have been taken by surprise – even Richard didn't have any concrete idea of what would happen next. The second time they must have been expecting it to happen. BJ Cole doesn't think they were making real plans to start a new band at Slane Castle. "Musicians, when they meet other musicians, they always talk about other projects outside of what they're currently doing but that doesn't mean to say that indicated a break-up," he says.

More rumours began circling when a classified advertisement

appeared in *NME* looking for a singer and a drummer for 'John Squire's Skunk Works Project'. It soon became apparent that the ex-Stone Roses guitarist was now playing with Simon Jones. John Squire had forged a relatively successful career after the Stone Roses with his new band The Seahorses, having big hits with 'Love Is The Law' and 'Blinded By The Sun'. In 1999, though, he'd parted company with The Seahorses' vocalist Chris Helme and they'd ended up scrapping their putative second album and breaking up the band.

The new project was intended to consist of a young, unknown vocalist Duncan Baxter, John Squire, Simon Jones and John's old drummer from the Seahorses, Mark Heaney. They rehearsed together for eight months and came up with six songs before something went wrong. "It just wasn't happening for me… I just had a nasty gut feeling about it all," Simon Jones said later.

John Squire was based up in the North West of England while, by then, Simon was living in London so there were always going to be logistical problems. "I didn't feel I had a life outside going up to John's and musically it wasn't 100% satisfying for me," he said. "It's nothing to do with John or who John is or what he does musically – it was just a personal thing for me that I wasn't into it."

There was also the central issue at the heart of The Verve's break-up. Having achieved a certain level of success, none of the members felt the need to compromise. They now had the freedom to do whatever they wanted and Simon was determined to make the kind of music that he was into, rather than follow the lead of another dominant character.

When they started The Verve, they all liked many of the same bands, Can, Funkadelic, The Stooges, Stone Roses. They all loved the same dirty rock 'n' roll sound. As time went on, though, they began pulling in different directions. They also had much more confidence in their own abilities and less willingness to compromise. Simon Jones decided to put together a new band, with Simon Tong and Duncan Baxter, down in London. They were called The Shining.

"Personally I feel much more at home with the music I'm playing," Simon Jones said in one of The Shining's first interviews with Roger Morton of the *NME*. "What I can say is that The Verve were going off in a direction of strings and ballads, and that's not where I was coming from at all. Loud guitars is it for me, and that's where I've got back to."

The Shining's debut album, *True Skies*, appeared in 2002 and showed some similarities to early Verve in the way that Duncan's vocals roamed loosely over a powerful groove. Despite receiving good reviews, though, it quickly disappeared.

Nick McCabe, meanwhile, was in no hurry to join another band. Along with Simon Jones and Simon Tong, he was commissioned to work on the soundtrack for the film of Iain Banks' *Complicity* but for various reasons much of their work was not used. After that he was mostly content to record his own ambient, electronic works with no concrete plans to ever release them.

Much later he contributed his guitar playing to an album by his hero John Martyn and worked with popular Liverpool band The Music, but he seemed scarred by his experiences with the music industry. His heroes now were people like Brian Eno who somehow seemed to have escaped the traditional band treadmill to do exactly what they wanted.

The only member of the band who Richard seemed keen to work with was Pete Salisbury. The moment he broke up the band, he was already forming plans for his first solo album. "Richard rang me and said that it's not happening," says BJ Cole of The Verve's split, "but that he was going to do a solo album and would I like to be involved."

CHAPTER 14

ALONE WITH EVERYBODY

Richard had been thinking about his solo career since 1996 when The Verve broke up the first time. He even wrote what would be his first single, 'A Song For The Lovers', that year. He started writing more songs not long after Slane Castle and things accelerated from there.

"Within about two days," he told Darren Taylor, "I was in a room with a desk just writing songs, doing it. Once I started it's like: 'These songs are happening!' All of a sudden the imagination's going, the first domino's gone and I'm off. The next minute I'm in Olympic Studios and I've got the fucking flautist going and the horn players and I'm making another record. As soon as I start it I can't stop!"

The sense of euphoria and freedom that he always had upon starting a record was even more pronounced than usual. He didn't have anybody else to hide behind but he didn't have to take responsibility for anybody else either. In The Verve he'd been the one who took the responsibility for doing the interviews, presenting himself as the face of the band. "I always had that weight," he said to *Planet Rock*. "I always took it, so it's less now. The weight of responsibility is just for me."

But that doesn't mean it was just him on the record. Initially he was sat in a recording studio with only his wife Kate and producer Chris Potter but, almost immediately, he set out on a kind of *Magnificent Seven* style search for musicians who could make his dream a reality. Except there wouldn't be seven of them. The liner notes for his first solo album would reveal that 22 people had played on it – and that doesn't include the London Gospel Choir or the London Session Orchestra.

He already had the keystone – Pete Salisbury – the man BJ Cole had described as "the rock" of The Verve. BJ Cole was lined up to play pedal steel and so he just needed a bass player. The seven million sales of *Urban Hymns* meant that there was no shortage of candidates even though he had a very specific idea of the kind of player he was looking for. He wanted his solo record to have more of a soulful quality than The Verve's albums and, because he didn't have a traditional lead guitarist, he also needed a bass player who could do more than just provide the rhythm. His answer was a Welsh session musician called Pino Palladino.

Pino had made his name in the Eighties working with Gary Numan, Paul Young and Tears For Fears among many others. By the late Nineties his laidback style had brought him to the attention of American stars such as Erykah Badu, Common, Talib Kweli and De La Soul. Richard had heard him on R&B singer D'Angelo's acclaimed *Voodoo* album and been highly impressed.

"Pino's a great professional," says BJ Cole. "He's one of the great session bass players. He's unique. His groove is fantastic. He produces one of the best grooves of any bass player I know and he's worked in all sorts of genres doing the same thing. He's just class. You pay a lot of money for somebody like that and the record sounds more expensive thanks to them!"

This may have been what Richard wanted but he was aware of the danger that a collection of session musicians would lack the intangible vibe of a real band. When they went into the studio, his main concern was in making them express themselves beyond merely playing to order.

"In the studio there was a great band," BJ Cole says. "It was Pino Palladino and Richard on guitar and Sobbo and me. And a guy called Steve Sidelnyk who programmed some of the drum stuff. There was a long process of evolving Richard's song ideas. That was a great process to be involved with."

From Richard's point of view, the joy of working with musicians like BJ Cole and Pino Palladino was that they were extremely talented and yet their whole focus was on realising his ideas. He could simply hum a vague bassline and Pino would be able to grasp what he wanted immediately. The other difference was that there was none of the baggage that The Verve had accumulated through their school days, long tours in beaten-up vans and the pressures of eventual success.

"I think I've felt more secure making this record," he said to Lily Moayeri of website *drdrew.com*, "because no one could come into the creative environment and dislodge it and send it in a different direction."

Needless to say, his new band didn't spend large chunks of studio time off their faces on ecstasy, either. There were new outside influences creeping in this time. During the recording of the album, Richard discovered that Kate was pregnant. In terms of his songwriting this would have more impact on later records – *Human Conditions* and *Keys To The World* – than it would on his debut solo album (to be called *Alone With Everybody*), but it still added to the feelings of rebirth and positivity that surrounded the sessions. Richard and Kate were actually living at the studio at the time because the house they'd bought wasn't finished. Nevertheless the atmosphere was the happiest it had been since the first few weeks of *A Northern Soul*. In the past, even his happier songs were often haunted by regrets or fears for the future but this time he made a conscious decision to turn away from nihilism.

"I love Curtis Mayfield and Al Green," he said, "and a lot of the music I love celebrates life. I touched on that with 'Lucky Man' on the last album but I just wanted an album that was more rounded. I wanted a tune that gives you your first time in New York."

His first single as a solo artist, *A Song For The Lovers*, was another of Richard's ambiguous love songs. It sounds, as BJ Cole suggested, even more plush and expensive than anything on *Urban Hymns*. His vocal is clean and flawless and from the opening burst of strings onwards it's pitched in exactly the same place, somewhere between trepidation and euphoria, as 'Sonnet' or 'Lucky Man'. Starting by describing him searching for his insides in a hotel room it isn't the simple paean to his relationship with Kate that the title might suggest.

Instead, there's a lot of fear and sadness mixed in with the warm sentiment of the title. When he asks the DJ to play a song for his lover, it sounds like he's worried about what will happen if he doesn't. The strings follow this model, alternately surging upwards, bright and euphoric, or swooping downwards and sounding melancholy and dramatic.

And, although his is the only voice on the single, in places he duets with himself, giving it an expansive feel that's influenced by the records he loved by Marvin Gaye and Al Green, proving once again that he was one of the best rock vocalists of the Nineties.

"I thought Richard's abilities as a singer came through better on that album than they did with The Verve," BJ Cole says. "I know he was criticised by many people but I thought that it was a fantastic album. I've worked with many great singers – David Sylvian, Scott Walker and people like that. As a rock 'n' roll singer, he's way above the quality of most people that front rock 'n' roll bands. He's heading in that direction. He's much better than people think he is."

When they finished the album, Richard encountered a problem he'd never had before. He couldn't think of a name for the record. John Best helped him out with the first two Verve albums and *Urban Hymns* came to him easily but as the release date loomed he was still stumped. "I'm normally good at titles," he joked, "but my son arrived at the same time and he needed a name as well so two in one month was too much!"

Eventually he scanned through a pile of books on his desk until he came upon a book of Charles Bukowski's poems. The first one that caught his eye was called *Alone With Everybody*. It might have seemed a slightly inappropriate title for a record that was so determinedly turning its back on nihilism. The poem is about the impossibility of ever finding real love. Graveyards are slowly filling up, Bukowski suggests bleakly, but nothing can ever fill the spiritual hole inside of us. What's more Bukowski was the archetypal artist-as-waster, supposedly only interested in dividing his time between drinking, womanising and writing. That, too, was a long way from Richard's new life.

But when the album opened with the strings for 'A Song For The Lovers', they practically screamed, like 'Bitter Sweet Symphony' at the start of *Urban Hymns,* that this was an important, serious album. As one of several songs that Richard had written at the same time as tracks from *Urban Hymns*, it was also designed to make the point that this wasn't any great change of direction. That, he was now saying, was almost a Richard Ashcroft album and this was just the next step on the road he'd been going down since *History*. With its repeated refrain of the Wilson Pickett song title "In the midnight hour" on the outro, it also explicitly connected him with soul music rather than the indie he'd been associated with in the past.

The second track, 'I Get My Beat', was one he kept going back to in interviews. It seems to have been the song he was most proud of for the way it escaped the usual clichés of 'alternative' music.

"It could be an Irish folk song, it could be Curtis Mayfield, it could be Burt Bacharach, it could be Morricone," he said to Darren Taylor. "With so much of what's considered alternative music now, it's easy to pin-point references and say this is another version of something. With a bit of confidence and imagination it's twisting now into my own sound and my own vibe."

The Irish element comes across most strongly in the flute that snakes through the background of the song but the strongest part is, once again, the strings and Richard's slow, portentous vocal. It lacks much of a chorus and relies more upon the pleasant smoothness of the overall sound. There's a huge amount going on, with The London Gospel Choir chipping in towards the end and a saxophone solo coming out of nowhere, but it's all so lushly produced that Richard's description of the song as a massive culture-clash isn't entirely plausible.

The next track, 'Brave New World', is equally smooth and equally dependent on the strings and some woozy lovelorn pedal steel from BJ Cole. With its heat-haze sound and mystical lyrics, it's the closest thing on the record to the jams of the early Verve but in a much less ferocious form. It's space rock of a kind but done in a much gentler, softer way.

By now the fears of some Verve fans would have been confirmed. There might have been a number of new styles on his first solo album but rock didn't seem to be one of them. However 'New York' raises the tempo. Starting with an almost ominous sound of sirens and bleeps, it quickly builds into one of his most optimistic, exuberant songs. The chorus essentially just repeats a variation on the title over and over but the insistent way he sings it, along with a rolling bassline from Pino Palladino, gives it an urgency that the album needed after the laidback vibe of the first three tracks. The energy and chaos of the song really does sound like the city, just as it was intended.

But after that, 'You On My Mind In My Sleep' slides back into sleepy ballad territory. This is probably the most countrified song on the album. BJ Cole's pedal steel is at its most traditional and Richard's lyric is straight out of the Nashville school of songwriting. Then Wil Malone's string arrangement rises up out of the mix and a low, groaning guitar sound breaks out. Leaving well alone is clearly not on the agenda. Any rough edges have been knocked off and the idea that less might, just possibly, be more doesn't seem to have been considered. Despite this, his gift with melody is still very much apparent.

The next track, 'Crazy World', spirals upwards again with some winningly ominous pedal steel and a powerful, exclamatory vocal. The only real problem with it is that the clichéd lyrics don't work with the insistent and somewhat self-important tone. The idea that the world is, hey, a bit mad, isn't original or interesting enough to bear the weight of the powerful music. It's about "a modern-day Bonnie and Clyde," Richard said but this doesn't come across very effectively. Still, if you can ignore what he's singing about, the weirdly distorted guitar sound that comes in does give the record a welcome touch of roughage.

After that, 'On A Beach' sends the album back into a blissful sleep. It starts like 'Lucky Man' on tranquillisers and the title makes perfect sense. It's a song where you can almost hear a sunny beach holiday in BJ Cole's guitar sound. Perhaps fortunately Richard doesn't sing like he's determined that the listener should hear every word, too. For the first time, the vocal is just another instrument, rather as it was on *A Storm In Heaven*. Like 'Brave New World' this is another step back into space.

The second single from the album, 'Money To Burn', is much more straightforwardly upbeat, unusually so for a song that uses pedal steel so extensively. Instead, BJ Cole's laidback riffs sound slightly cheeky, like a whoopee cushion going off in slow motion as Richard's vocal woah-yeahs its way through an unambiguous but not very likeable love song. The problem might be that the central metaphor, of having loads of money and wanting to spend it on the person you love in the short time before you die, isn't all that endearing.

The positivity that Richard had talked about does come across in 'Money To Burn'. The playing is, unsurprisingly, technically brilliant, with all the different elements meshing perfectly but this, too, takes away some of the grit that The Verve had. You can almost smell the expensive studio. The ability that he now had to put absolutely everything he wanted into a song – the country guitar of BJ Cole, the sinuous bass of Pino Palladino and every element of an orchestra – was perhaps not always a benefit.

On *Urban Hymns*, when he piled on different instruments and sounds they ran into each other, creating a solid whole. On 'Money To Burn', the production is so clean that every element stands out bright and clear as though it had been thoroughly scrubbed that morning.

After that, 'Slow My Heart' inevitably slows things down dramatically with some more countrified pedal steel and an emotional vocal. Although the first few songs were all similarly paced, by now the record's taken on the quality of a gentle roller-coaster; sleepy country ballads alternating with mid-tempo pop songs. They both have their good points and 'Slow My Heart' has a particularly strong vocal performance. Richard avoids over emphasising each word and this makes him sound much less strident and brash than he occasionally could.

'C'Mon People (We're Making It Now)', then, suddenly whooshs back upwards. The third single from the record, it's much better than 'Money To Burn', even though it has perhaps been over-polished in the studio. It has an obvious soul influence, starting by sounding like 'Reach Out (I'll Be There)' by The Four Tops but the loping, effects-treated guitar riff puts it firmly into what American radio programmers call "adult contemporary" territory.

Then the last track, 'Everybody', slides back down again, literally, with a liberal application of BJ Cole's pedal steel. It's another song that takes Nashville as its starting point before swelling back upwards towards an epic climax that then slowly ebbs away with dignified grandeur. Like the beginning of the album, the end signifies that we're listening to something important and momentous. At this point, coming off the back of a previous album that had been so successful, Richard Ashcroft's confidence in his artistic powers couldn't have been higher. It was a confidence that the album's reception might dent, just slightly, but it couldn't altogether destroy.

When the album came out, 'A Song For The Lovers' did pretty well, reaching number three in the UK charts and when *Alone With Everybody* came out, it went straight in at number one. However, Richard was disappointed that it didn't quite reach the heights of *Urban Hymns*. Later on he would bemoan the fact that six million fans disappeared because he'd changed "brand names" from The Verve to Richard Ashcroft.

"I lost six million people because I was no longer The Verve," he said to Tom Lanham of American paper the *Oakland Tribune*, "so I lived through the fact that, on a professional and artistic level, we really just deal in trade names." There may be some truth in this, but it may have just been that nothing on *Alone With Everybody* reached the heights of 'The Drugs Don't Work' or 'Bitter Sweet Symphony'. "It's that age old thing of band chemistry," says Roger Morton. "You split people up and put them on their own and, guess what, it doesn't work."

Richard talked in interviews about being the exception to the rule that all singers who break away from successful bands must, inevitably, be a diminished force. Yet he knew enough rock history to recognise that the odds were against him. He was a huge fan of The Beatles and he was well aware of their difficult solo careers.

Most of the reviews remained pretty positive. *NME* approvingly described *Alone With Everybody* as a "60 minute torrent of positivity" and "an open love letter to his wife."

And *Spin* magazine's Carrie Havranek agreed with Richard's assertion that it was simply a continuation of what he'd been doing for several years. "Although the band split up for good in April last year, there's no huge loss, as there's no appreciable difference in the music," she said "*Alone With Everybody* is, well, just like the Verve, only more sedate, a bit wiser, and a little less prone to psychedelic jamming."

But there were dissenting voices. *Select* said that it was "often closer to Elton John than The Verve". In *The Face*, Craig McLean summarised one of the most common – and churlish – criticisms of his new solo direction – that he'd lost his edge because he was now too contented in his personal life.

"Given the power he found in the shadows he tapped into when looking for a way out of the murk (of drugs, amongst other things), it's hard to have to lose him to the light," he said. "Love and peace have replaced restlessness and mystery."

Inevitably Richard paid more attention to the criticism than to the applause. Certainly the album didn't get the reception that he'd hoped but the six million disappearing fans probably hurt him more than the reviews. At the Manchester date of the first tour following its release, he snapped, "This is for all of you that are still here. Don't believe the hype … I haven't got my pipe and slippers."

At times his psyche seemed like a metal can that could take vicious dents but still spring back into its old shape. The relative failure of *Alone With Everybody* surprised him and made him briefly despondent but he still believed that he could take things back to The Verve's level. He never lost faith in his artistic abilities and, when he spoke to Darren Taylor in 2000, he was confident that commercially he was still a force to be reckoned with, too. Although he'd once been happy having nowhere to live and no shoes on his feet, he had developed a piratical joy at forcing his label and publishing backers to pay him what he was worth. "I'm the best fucking songwriter on the whole roster without a shadow of a fucking doubt," he said.

Unfortunately, a very difficult period followed when he parted ways with manager Jazz Summers and lawyers became involved; a fairly bleak spell of legal arguments was eventually resolved with some satisfaction on both sides because nine years later, when The Verve would reform again, Jazz was once more their manager.

Richard had better news later that year when *Alone With Everybody* was nominated for the Mercury Prize and was immediately made second favourite by the bookies. It didn't win (the prize went to Badly Drawn Boy's *The Hour Of Bewilderbeast*) but it was a reminder that not everybody had written him off since he'd left his band.

Still, the loss of Jazz came at a bad time. One of the main reasons he'd employed the Big Life management team in the first place was because he wanted The Verve to break America. There, casual rock fans were vaguely aware of 'Bitter Sweet Symphony' but that was about it. He wasn't exactly starting again from scratch but he'd certainly dropped a few rungs on the ladder. It just meant he needed to tour the clubs again but, with the number of people who'd played on the record, that was no easy undertaking. The only advantage for Richard Ashcroft was that he no longer had to carry around the baggage of ten years of The Verve. In some ways this made his first tour much easier.

"I toured *Alone With Everybody* a lot more than I did with The Verve," BJ Cole says, "and it was great. We all got on really well and he was a great frontman. There was a different dynamic than to The Verve tour. There was no way you could make it as tight-knit as they had all been because they'd known each other at school. But it must be difficult when you're working with your schoolmates and a rift that probably goes back to your school days pulls you apart. It must be difficult to keep something like that together. If you've grown up as schoolkids together and then you fall apart it must be a major blow."

His first date as a solo artist took place at Ted's Wrecking Yard in Toronto in front of an invited audience of about 200 American and Canadian journalists. It was the day before he was due to film the 'Money To Burn' video in Manhattan. The video once again featured him just walking along a crowded street but this time he generously gestured to people to go in front of him, instead of just bumping into them and knocking them down.

It was a level of politeness that might have been hard to sustain as he spent most of the day in the street from half eight in the morning onwards. That night he played again, in front of another music industry crowd at Joe's Pub in New York. According to the *NME* he was exhausted but on good form. "How many records do you think this will sell?" he asked a photographer, pointing to the bags under his eyes.

The next date couldn't have been more of a contrast – a headline slot at the V Festival. After The Verve's disappointing appearance in 1998, without Nick McCabe, as the band slowly crumbled, it was his chance to show that he was better off alone (he played both nights, Saturday in Staffordshire and Sunday in Chelmsford). At Chelmsford, noticing that Moby appeared to be drawing a bigger crowd, he quipped, "Maybe I should do a few fuckin' car adverts!" But by performing acoustic versions of songs like 'History' alongside new songs like 'A Song For The Lovers', he was able to make the point that they were both written entirely by the same hand.

Steadily growing in confidence he dedicated the next single, 'C'Mon People ('We're Making It Now)' to Liam Gallagher, "the greatest rock and roll star this country's ever produced", and finished with a version of 'Bitter Sweet Symphony', which was as awe-inspiring as ever. "Finally, with the last kick of the match, V2000 has witnessed a true star," proclaimed *NME*.

'C'Mon People (We're Making It Now)' was released on his 29th birthday in September 2000. It was no surprise when it followed the same pattern as the first two singles, peaking a little lower at twenty one in the charts and then quickly disappearing.

After the festival season, things once again dropped down a notch when he left the UK to tour Europe. Although The Verve had been huge pretty much everywhere, the audiences were much smaller for his solo gigs. When he got to Sweden in September 2000 Richard couldn't hide his disappointment.

"I bet if we were here with the name The Verve there would have been another ten thousand people," he said. "We're playing the same songs you know. But you are the faithful, you have seen through all the shit, thank you."

Nevertheless the atmosphere on the tour was good and Richard was popular with most of the musicians he worked with. "Generally people who do well and are successful over a long period of time are quite nice," says saxophonist Tim Sanders. "The people who aren't, nobody wants to work with and it's that much harder for them to make progress. A lot of the big names we've worked for have teams that go back years and years," he continues. "It's a collaborative artform and you have to know how to collaborate and get on with people. The stories of people who are arseholes are entertaining but they're few and far between in my experience."

That year Richard also confirmed that his name still had some cachet when he supported Madonna at a small gig (for her) at London's Brixton Academy. Madonna has an unerring instinct for seizing on whatever happens to be cool but it was to prove another difficult experience. Madonna's fans weren't interested in listening to any of his solo material and only old hits like 'The Drugs Don't Work' made any impact at all.

Then at a Birmingham gig in December, he somehow managed to fall off the stage, breaking his ribs. It was, typically, right before the start of a full American tour. It had almost become a tradition in The Verve that somebody had to break a bone immediately before they were due to go to America and it seemed like he was going to continue the voodoo on his solo career. Luckily he didn't have to cancel any dates and the tour (which had, anyway, been rescheduled from November because of illness) was well received.

It must have been glaringly apparent to him, though, that he was once again playing venues like St Andrew's Hall in Detroit, which he used to play in the pre-*Urban Hymns* era of The Verve. He also found himself having to push his band to stretch the songs beyond their recorded version. He wasn't used to playing with musicians who played everything note-perfect as it was on the record.

Then, in the autumn of 2000, he went to Japan for the first time, something he'd never even done with The Verve. He was disappointed at the reception. It's become a cliché of even relatively obscure British bands that when they go to Japan they're mobbed by fans at the airport or the hotel. This didn't happen to Richard.

"There were a few fans waiting here and there but not mobs of them, no," says BJ Cole. "Maybe that's what he wanted and he didn't get it! The only time I thought Richard wasn't able to cope with the situation was the week in Japan," BJ continues. "He didn't like Japan at all. The Japanese audiences are very polite and they don't say anything during the songs and they applaud quietly at the end of songs and that's not the way that Richard works. He likes to rabble rouse. Get the audience going. And he couldn't do it. I think that threw him somewhat. It was obvious that he wasn't enjoying it as he normally does. I think he needs the energy of the crowd to do the show. That's part of the chemistry, to get a good performance and a good singing performance – he needs feedback."

In Osaka he rechristened 'Brave New World' 'Jet Lag Blues' and the *NME* reviewer, who was evidently a fan, commented: "It proves to be a deflatingly honest appraisal of the state of play. It's hard not to expect something exceptional every time sets of this calibre are presented. This, however, is Richard Ashcroft's off night and the disappointment is almost palpable."

There were many more dates right the way through to 2002, most of them much more enthusiastically received, but Richard's pride was hurt. In February 2002, at a Brixton Academy gig, wearing an Elvis-style combination of white leather jacket and white flares, he thanked the crowd for, "not believing the bullshit about me and my music. We've got a long way to go, a whole lot of tunes so stick with us," he promised.

Characteristically his downbeat mood wouldn't last long.

CHAPTER 15

HUMAN BEHAVIOUR

"I've got some amazing things planned for the next album," Richard told writer Darren Taylor after *Alone With Everybody* was finished. "This next one will be the best record I've ever made. It will be one of those records that I'm going to find difficult to ever match because I've gathered the means and the characters, I want to get Money Mark down for the next one, I want to get [DJ] Shadow down, fuse them in with the pedal steel. I've got the basic structures for, I think, a very powerful record."

Although he put a brave face on the modest impact of *Alone With Everybody*, Richard was disappointed that it didn't simply carry on where *Urban Hymns* had left off in commercial terms. As far as he was concerned, he'd written 'A Song For The Lovers' and 'The Drugs Don't Work' in the same burst of creativity. He'd even hired a supremely accomplished band to play the new songs.

Changes were afoot. For the second album he dispensed with the services of BJ Cole. "I was a bit sad that I wasn't involved in an on-going way after the first album because I thought we had quite a strong connection," says BJ. No official reason was given as to why he wasn't required but then he'd always been aware, even when he worked with The Verve, that he wasn't joining anything officially. That was the nature of being a session musician.

That was something that Richard had started to have more experience of, too. Just as he had for UNKLE back in 1997, he provided another excellent vocal performance-for-hire to the Chemical Brothers on their *Come With Us* album. He'd first met them at the aftershow party for one of Oasis's early gigs. They were DJing but he was intent on getting Wayne Griggs on the decks. But, as he listened to what they were playing, he started getting sucked in despite himself.

"I was caught between a rock and a hard place, to get these guys off who we didn't know and to get our guy on, or leave them on and keep listening to this amazing music they were playing," he told Canadian magazine *JAM Showbiz*. "That was the first meeting, and it was a bit surreal."

After that, a mutual friend kept bugging him to do something with the Brothers and eventually he agreed. They sent him a tape and, just as he had with the DJ Shadow track, he simply listened to that for a couple of weeks and then went into the studio and provided an entirely improvised vocal performance on the spot. "I had absolutely no idea what the words were going to be until I opened my mouth," he told *Jam*. "I find that is a real big buzz."

The resulting tune, 'The Test', benefited from one of his rawest, most ragged performances. It was almost as though everything he'd been keeping in on the tasteful, expensively produced *Alone With Everybody* album was suddenly let out. It started with him calling out to God in a voice which sounded much older and more pinched than it ever had before. The effect was pure blues, like Moby's *Play* album set on fire and blasted into space.

It would have been interesting if he'd done a whole album like that but instead the next long player, *Human Conditions*, was another attempt to create something classic and simple. He'd been listening to a lot of mellow music from the early Seventies and he wanted to capture a similar vibe – the calm after the storm.

"I went through my 'Sixties' [in] the late Nineties, with all the madness that brought," he told *Jam*. "But I am still on this earth, on this rock, trying to make sense of it, trying to get through this life, and trying to be an all right person. That is how it is, man."

Nevertheless, despite his admiration of a simpler, more mellow kind of music, there was no question of going back to a basic studio set up. After making records on a relative shoestring in the early years of Verve, he relished his newly elastic budget. "They're going to give me a large amount of money to make my next record, guaranteed, whatever happens to this one," he laughed to Darren Taylor after *Alone With Everybody*. "Which to me is hilarious!"

This is borne out by *Human Conditions* complex gestation. It was recorded at Astoria, Real World, Metropolis and Olympic Studios with another large cast of players. Money Mark and DJ Shadow weren't involved but he did have Talvin Singh who'd been one of the most acclaimed new talents of the end of the Nineties. Talvin won the 1999 Mercury Prize for his album *OK,* which fused electronic and traditional Indian music in a new form the press dubbed tablatronics. Talvin played on four tracks on the new album and he was just one of 12 people who would make an appearance, again not including the choir or the orchestra.

Once again if Richard's confidence had been dented by the criticism he received, it didn't stop him expecting the impossible. More pertinently it didn't stop him from actually making the impossible happen. Only he could listen to a demo and wonder out loud whether Brian Wilson of the Beach Boys might like to sing on it. Brian was one of his all-time heroes and he had spent long hours trying to work out how he created the sounds that he made.

"With the limited equipment they had then, he still brought out this incredible music when people at that time were struggling to get these sounds," he enthused in an interview with *Mojo* magazine.

The Beach Boys' *Pet Sounds* and Dennis Wilson's *Pacific Ocean Blue* were two records that he'd listened to obsessively ever since his teens. But in 2000, Brian had only recently started a slow recovery from the mental illness he'd suffered from for decades. It was clearly ridiculous that he would sing on the solo album of a British artist he'd probably never heard of.

"I just got that feeling that it should happen," Richard told *VH1.* "Call it daydreaming or visualisation. All you do is oil the cogs. You make it easier to happen, but you don't make it happen." This was the belief in positive visualisation that he'd had since his stepfather had taught him about the Rosicrucians. And, somehow, it worked.

"I had this daydream listening to 'Nature Is The Law' thinking, *It would be great if Brian Wilson could sing on this,"* he said to Gary Crowley. "Two days later I'm doing a photoshoot, somebody knows Brian's manager's number. The call's made – he's gonna do it!"

To give him credit, Richard sounds genuinely astonished when he recounts this story. He sent Brian Wilson a tape with no instructions as to what he should do with it ("Grasshopper doesn't give advice to the master, man", he said) and a few days later he got something back. "I was convinced somebody was going to put a spanner in the works at some point, something was going to go wrong," he said to *Planet Rock*. "There'll be a powercut when he sits down at the piano."

But there was no powercut. Brian received the lyric and went into his studio in Los Angeles. Not long afterwards he sent the recording back to the UK, having added a series of chain-gang style chants to the end of the track. When Richard received the tape, he said, "it was one of the greatest moments of my life."

Despite his everlasting reserves of self-belief, there was more humility in the lyrics that he was now writing than there had been on *Alone With Everybody*. Maybe it was because of the relative failure of his debut compared with The Verve or maybe it was just the new anxiety in his life that came from being a father. He also said in a radio interview that marriage had done a good job of bringing him joltingly down to Earth.

"The great thing about being married is that it destroys your ego," he said to Clint Boon. "My wife destroys my ego everyday and that's beautiful because if my ego got away with itself, I wouldn't be where I am today."

He told Sylvia Patterson in *The Guardian* that the new record was about "the vulnerability of being a father and the vulnerability of the world. It's seeing beauty, but also having an awareness of your place in the universe and how you deal with that."

Since Sonny was born, he'd had to reassess his place in the universe and the events of his 30th birthday accelerated that process. He turned 30 on September 11, 2001, and he'd gone to his mother-in-law's house in the South of France to celebrate when his father-in-law rang and told them to put the TV on. What he saw, the twin towers in New York collapsing, affected him as it did anybody who'd visited the city. Ever since that first trip, driving around Times Square playing 'Man Called Sun', he'd always felt like it was a kind of spiritual home. He said to Tom Lanham, "it put me into a very depressed state for quite a long time. Because I suddenly realised that the decisions that were going to be made by the administrations in America and England were not only going to affect my life, they were going to affect my son's life, and his son's as well."

That might sound like retrospective wisdom but it was deeply meant. His whole ethos after the collapse of The Verve involved turning away from nihilism and trying to promote a more positive world view. After September 11 and the wars that followed, this became harder and harder to maintain.

"Over the past five to six years, I've spent that time learning how to rebuild my life again," he said to Corey duBrowa much later. He realised that this could sound narcissistic and perhaps it was. He admitted that he hadn't suffered in the way that so many other people had but he'd always been prone to melancholia, even depression. As somebody who thought in 1999 that things were improving for him personally, and for the world at large, it was hard for him to cope with the fact that things hadn't gone according to plan for either.

In this climate, music became even more important. "We all have our daily prescription of yoga, football, religion, or whatever gets us through that day," he said to Sylvia Patterson. "My thing is music. It's the only thing that gives me a sense of calm and balance. It's the thing I know I'm good at."

Another thing that touched him deeply was the death of George Harrison in November 2001. Richard was almost as upset as he'd been when John Lennon died. He even wrote an obituary for *The Independent* which made it clear where a lot of his inspiration for writing about "peace and love" had come from. "These ideals are easy to mock," he said, "but I wouldn't want to be living in a world in which no one was spreading that message."

As he went on, he could easily have been talking about himself. "It is easy to forget how young he was when it all started," he continued, "but he came to terms quickly with the plastic nature of the music industry. I guess it frightened him but he was not addicted to the bullshit as so many of them were. He came to terms with it, and looked at it with his wry, cracked slant."

He would need a "wry, cracked slant" himself when the new record came out but it wasn't the 'disaster' that it's occasionally been dubbed. It was just very low-key and somewhat lightweight. 'Check The Meaning' was an even more laid-back opening to an album than 'A Song For The Lovers' had been. It sounds weary. It doesn't sound like he's preparing to blow his detractors away. It's more like he's resignedly exhorting his critics to pay attention to what he's saying for once, with no real expectation that they will.

Then 'Buy It In Bottles' slows things down even further. Despite this, it contained some of his best moments since 'A Song For The Lovers'. It starts out as a slow ballad in the vein of 'The Drugs Don't Work' and it might have been even better if he had kept faith with nothing except the combination of a great vocal performance and some simply strummed guitar. There was far more emotion in his voice than on most of his other solo singles. It was the kind of song that you could imagine country singers like Gram Parsons or Jimmy Webb singing. It was his attempt at a 'Wichita Lineman', a song that would rise from a humble base into something soaring and powerful.

Initially the strings are relatively restrained, too. They walk step by step with the vocal giving it just enough of that luxurious feel that he liked so much. Unfortunately, towards the end of the song, more and more elements are piled on. The strings get louder, slide guitar takes over from his acoustic and he almost has to shout to make himself heard over the top.

The next track, 'Bright Lights', was the only song on the album to contain a slight nod to 2001's dominant, New York–inspired garage rock sound (The Strokes *et al*). For a few seconds, it's even slightly reminiscent of the cult classic 'Roadrunner' by Jonathan Richman, which was such a key tune to garage rock fans. Then the squalling guitar drops away to allow Richard's vocals to take up more space with a ranting lyric about city life and mental illness. It's a long way removed from the kind of tunes that are most often associated with his solo career. There's no real structure to it. A kind of chorus comes in at one point but it's abandoned in favour of a rolling cacophony and an extended outro.

'Paradise' quickly gets things back on to more familiar ground with a lovely, haunting trumpet and a bluesy, beaten-down vocal. When it gets going, it sounds like it's going to turn into 'Belfast Child' by Simple Minds. Like 'Buy It In Bottles', it might have been better with fewer components. The gospel choir and the orchestra are beautiful but you do get the feeling that having the money, the talent available and the time to do whatever he wanted wasn't always good for Richard's creativity.

The next track, 'God In The Numbers', posed the difficult question of what kind of music do you write for a song with such an esoteric subject matter. It was about Richard's belief that, one day, mathematicians would find a formula that proved the existence of God as a kind of all-encompassing spirit in the universe. The answer is some sonorous organ, emotive keyboard sounds from Kate and a vocal which evokes the sound of a mouse snoring in a church. It has the same strengths and weaknesses of many of the songs on *Human Conditions*. It's got a lush, velvety sound and all of the elements, not least Richard's voice, are on top form but there's no real hook. There is a chorus but it's slow and gentle, barely noticeable.

The next track, 'Science Of Silence', at least tries to remedy that. Following 'Bitter Sweet Symphony', Richard had sworn to write his own symphonies, something better than Jagger, Richards, Andrew Loog Oldham and his orchestra could manage. 'Science Of Silence' might be what he meant. Built around grandiose strings, it's certainly searching for the same classic, heavenly orchestra sound that 'Bitter Sweet Symphony' had. Wil Malone was still on-board conducting the London Session Orchestra and providing the same service that he had in the past – knowing just how far to take the strings without overpowering the song but giving it a plush, extravagant quality.

In 1991, though, when Wil's work helped make Massive Attack's 'Unfinished Sympathy' such an all-time classic, the style was original and fresh. By 2002, similar strings had been used many, many times before, not least by Richard Ashcroft.

'Science Of Silence' had the same theme as 'Check The Meaning' – how the love of his wife helped him deal with the essential insignificance of human existence in an uncaring universe. This time the tune was a little more upbeat, the chorus slightly stronger. His voice is still low and gruff but the ubiquitous strings are allowed to soar upwards. Like 'Check The Meaning', it's a pretty song but there's nothing about it to grab the attention. Still there was an underlying warmth to Richard's vocals which hadn't been there before when he was younger and cockier. The edge might have gone but there was a new smoothness and maturity.

It was all very pleasant but by 'Man On A Mission', the last remaining Verve fans still tuning in might have been wondering where the 'Rolling People's or 'Come On's were. 'Man On A Mission' has a Bruce Springsteen theme – the story of a young runaway – set to yet more gentle country rock and another swelling orchestra of strings. It's not hard to imagine how one of the big American country stars might have approached the same song; repeating the chorus and putting the vocals and guitar much higher in the mix. Richard's take on country is a lot more subtle. He's going for that heartstring-tugging Nashville sound but the structure of the song is much looser, with the outro once again taking up much of the running time. It means that it's never hard to listen to but there's nothing to make it memorable.

If anything 'Running Away' softens things even more. It never really gets going but the delicate piano and Talvin Singh's laidback beats make it one of the most affecting songs on the album. It's as though he's finding it too exhausting to arrange his music into anything approaching a song but then again all three albums by The Verve had songs that were just as spaced-out. If it had been on *Urban Hymns,* then, it would undoubtedly have been hugely acclaimed.

Then 'Lord I've Been Trying' brings back the Biblical, gospel feel. Opening with some of the most powerful strings on the record, it builds up with some squalling guitar and a vocal where Richard is crying out to God. One criticism of *Human Conditions* was that the songs are very unstructured and that's certainly true here. It seems like it should have been broken up into a traditional, verse, chorus, verse structure but that was never really Richard's way. He much preferred to loop sounds, scatting or ranting over a shifting bed of music without ever fixing on a hook. That always made him a welcome oddity in a predictable pop world.

The final song on the album, 'Nature Is The Law', almost seems to carry on where 'Lord I've Been Trying' leaves off. The strings have the same swooping quality and there's the same gospel feel with Richard singing in a deep, resonant voice like a modern day Paul Robeson. The extraordinary appearance of Brian Wilson on the track adds to this gospel feel as Brian adds his chain-gang chant.

Human Conditions is by no means a bad record. The problem was that having written songs like 'Bitter Sweet Symphony', 'The Drugs Don't Work' and 'Song For The Lovers', critics and fans expected tunes that were equally immediate. Instead much of the record entirely ignores pop music's normal responsibility to provide hooks and sudden dramatic changes of direction. The typical song on the record builds up slowly with strings and increasingly emotional vocals and then fades away over a long outro.

With the addition of Talvin Singh's Eastern percussion, the emotive sounds of the London Community Gospel Choir and the London Session Orchestra, he's created what he often rightly describes as a kind of soup of all his influences. But instead of the innovative sound he thought he'd achieve, he created something that was essentially easy listening. It's all very pleasant but in a year when the big sound was raw rock 'n' roll, it couldn't have been less cool.

But, despite the mellowness of the record, he was adamant that there was still a punk spirit in there somewhere. "I believe I'm punk rock," he said to *VH1*. "People might say 'What the fuck?' I don't necessarily mean how you sound on guitar. All these things are an expression of something that should be just instinctive and raw: Patty Smith had it, John Lydon had it, Liam Gallagher, Kurt Cobain, George Clinton had it."

This might have been true but very little of the spirit came across on record. Perhaps it got lost in the production process. Throughout Richard's career, even his most ardent fans have occasionally complained that the greatness of his live sets isn't always reflected in his recorded output.

"If I had put on fifteen stone and Kate had left and me and I'd almost OD'd on smack, then this record would have been received very well in my country," he complained wryly to Thomas Beller.

Which might well have been true but if all those things had happened he would probably have written a different album. 'Check The Meaning', the first single to be released prior to *Human Conditions*, was another step on the path he'd been on since *A Storm In Heaven* and it gave a good indication of where he was now coming from. On every record since then, one of his main objectives had been to express himself more clearly. Although there's a lot going on in 'Check The Meaning' — a sweet guitar melody, some subtle strings, low keyboard bleeps and a smooth rhythm — it's all there to complement and lift his vocal. Much more than on any of the tracks on *Alone With Everybody*, he sounds almost subdued, not sad exactly, but as though he's been through an awful lot and just about found something to cling to.

The title and the chorus literally implore the listener to pay attention to what he's saying but this might not have been such a good idea. Some critics accused him of arrogance for implying that what he was saying was hugely important. "Ashcroft carries on as if he were the first person in history to write a song about love," *The Guardian* complained.

In reality, the song was slightly more complicated than that. It seems to be about his realisation that there's no God and his belief that he's found the closest thing to God in his love for his wife. This attitude did, at least, have its roots in his essential good nature. He admired artists like John Lennon, George Harrison and others who had put out records with a consciously positive message. "I'm inspired by people like Brian Wilson and Pete Townshend who weren't afraid to talk about the power [that] pop can have on a mind," he said in an interview with *The Daily Record*.

In other interviews, he often went back to the idea that, in a world that was becoming increasingly divided, somebody had to sing about peace and love. He was fearful of the future of the planet, especially after the birth of his child, and he had the very laudable view that he should be doing his bit to make the world a better place. The only problem was that making the world a better place through a song's "message" is notoriously difficult. As film producer Sam Goldwyn said about films with something to say, "If you want to send a message, use Western Union."

Despite this, the gentleness of the song is highly appealing, at odds with the brashness of the chorus. In 2002 it was very different to everything else that was going on. Following the success of the The Strokes in 2000 the indie world had suddenly embraced garage rock. Bands like The Hives were now doing well and The Libertines were the critics' darlings. The popular new sound was raw and rough – a long way removed from the smooth mixture of country, rock and soul that Richard Ashcroft was putting out. Initially this didn't bother him.

"It's cool to be out of time," he said in an interview with Michael Devereaux of *Filter* magazine. "I think in this day and age, there's so much vying for your attention on a daily basis, it's kind of nice to have music you can swim in, you can float in, music that draws you in and has got more depth to it. The only thing with my music is, do people have time anymore to listen to music like that?"

The answer might have been 'no.' The song just didn't have the impact of his best work but neither was it the waste of space that his harshest critics claimed. In a way, Richard was his own worst enemy. Usually when artists are promoting a record they include endorsements from critics. 'Check The Meaning' had an endorsement, too, "the captain is back!" the promotional material claimed. The author of that statement was, of course, Richard Ashcroft. This kind of showmanship worked with big, bold songs like 'Bitter Sweet Symphony' and 'The Drugs Don't Work' but perhaps not with a low-key, pleasant tune like 'Check The Meaning'.

In the end, it did okay. Released in October 2002, it peaked at number eleven in the UK charts, proving that he still had a loyal fanbase, but it didn't make the kind of impact that Captain Rock thought he deserved. Still, despite his relative commercial comedown, he didn't need the acclaim of fans quite as much as he had in the past. Even more than music, the birth of Sonny had helped plug the gap that the death of his father had created. Sonny forced him to come down to Earth in a way that he'd never done before.

John Best remembers that, back in 1995, he was a likeable but not particularly useful house-guest. "He raids your underwear drawer because he doesn't own any underwear," John remembers. "Socks disappear. Pants disappear. I don't think he understands the concept of washing-up! He's not cleanliness obsessed. He's a nice young man on a one to one basis. Good conversationalist, interested in stuff, he's got an eager mind. He wants to *know* about stuff."

With a child around, though, Richard changed. He proudly told journalists that he'd spent long nights rocking Sonny to sleep after he was born. "I've only been away from Sonny for two nights in five and a half years," he told Siobhan Grogan of *Glamour* magazine much later. "I was very hands-on with him and used to rock him to sleep every night until I was drenched in sweat."

This didn't go down too well with the sections of the press that had originally seized on him as one of the last great rock stars. There was a feeling that he was living out another of the rock clichés – domesticity leading to creative impotence. His image wasn't helped by the fact that, far from being the freewheeling rebel of the past, he now lived in a mansion in the Gloucestershire countryside with dogs, chickens and peacocks. Even less 'cool', though, was his perceived domestic bliss with Kate and Sonny and certain writers were critical – a ludicrous and embarrassingly mean-spirited criticism. "I've joined the biggest club in the world," he said to Fiona Sturges at *The Independent*. "John Lennon had children, so did Bob Dylan and Kurt Cobain. Did they get taken apart for it? No!"

The next two singles from *Human Conditions* followed a very similar pattern to the ones from *Alone With Everybody*. 'Science Of Silence' peaked at number 14 and then 'Buy It In Bottles' reached number 26. Unfortunately, the album sold far fewer copies than *Alone With Everybody*. It was a real test of his new assertion that commercial success didn't mean much.

"Success is making the record," he told Darren Taylor, "success is waking up the next day looking at my wife and my son. People forget how successful it is just to finish a song, record it, it's there for life. What more do you want?"

The answer might be the same thing he'd always wanted, to make a difference and feel like his music was making its mark on the world. But after listening to *Human Conditions* it was almost hard to imagine that this was the same man who'd sang fierce songs like 'This Is Music' or exuded the irrepressible self-confidence of 'Bitter Sweet Symphony'. His solo work now seemed to exhibit a lack of any kind of jagged edge that might put casual listeners off. Maybe in his mind it seemed like the ideal listener wasn't the avid music fan who'd bought *A Northern Soul*, it was the great mass of people who might buy one or two records a year after hearing them on daytime radio. From a commercial point of view, one of his biggest problems was that there was now no rock 'n' roll story that his publicists could highlight to sell his records.

Music magazines are always desperate for an angle and in the past these had been easy to find. *A Storm In Heaven* was a debut album and the new is always exciting. When Verve first started to release singles, everybody who interviewed them was able to tell the story of 'Captain Rock' and his bunch of space cadets. Then when they came to *A Northern Soul*, there were even more stories to tell. The drugs. The odd behaviour. The tensions within the band and then the break-up and the eerie appropriateness of their 'last ever' single, 'History'.

So, from a marketing point of view, getting back together for *Urban Hymns* was genius, giving a further boost to The Verve's image as wayward, unpredictable visionaries. They needed great songs, of course, but it didn't hurt that they were able to present the world with such a classic rock 'n' roll image.

By the same token, breaking up again was also a huge attention grabber. Everybody was waiting to see what they would do next. The first solo album is always a big deal – a chance to see whether Richard was the true songwriting talent in the band, a chance to see whether he could hack it alone.

So what was *Human Conditions* then? It was just another album by singer-songwriter Richard Ashcroft, formerly of The Verve. There was no headline-grabbing angle it could be given. It was entirely resistant to hype and everything rested on the quality of the songs. If asked, Richard would probably say this was exactly what he wanted but in reality it meant that it got a few reviews, some critics liked it and some didn't, and that was it.

Although *Human Conditions* is often thought of as a critically slated record, that was by no means the case across the board. *Entertainment Weekly* declared that: "Though elaborately orchestrated, the songs retain their intimacy, communicated in Ashcroft's vocals, which, over the years, keep getting warmer."

And in the UK, *Mojo* agreed. "*Human Conditions* still somehow charms with its hungry troubadour's idealism," they said. His main problem was that some critics still saw signs of his new lifestyle in the music's mild, mellow character. "Good living has tilted his writing from surefooted and universal to numbing and platitudinous," said *Blender* magazine.

Perhaps even more significantly, his previous work had raised expectations to a level that was difficult to sustain. "*Human Conditions* is not a musical disaster on the scale of [Oasis's] *Heathen Chemistry*. It's just that, from Richard Ashcroft, more is expected," said Q magazine.

With characteristic defiance, he declared that in ten years people would realise that he was ahead of his time. The tsunami of Boxing Day 2004 seemed to bear out the message of 'Nature Is The Law' –

that the natural world is more powerful than man could ever be. He even said that had he released the song in 2005 critics would have accused him of cashing in on the tragedy (he was probably right).

But, more pertinently, he also made the point that the garage rock trend wouldn't be around forever. "Everything is very bombastic at the moment," he said to *VH1*, "everything is competing for your attention by being the loudest. So it's time to chill, give people the chance to swim in the music a little bit!" (an observation was proved correct by the increasing success of Coldplay and their ilk in the next few years).

Ultimately, *Human Conditions* would go gold in the UK, which wasn't bad, although *Alone With Everybody* had gone platinum. Outside the UK, though, there was little interest. The rest of the world didn't seem to know or care about his story and the songs, for all their low-key charm, didn't make a splash in the way that The Verve's classics had.

In October 2004, EMI released a Verve compilation album, *This Is Music: Singles 92-98,* which provided a harsh measure for his solo record. It was a strange turn-around. When The Verve presented their record label with freeform rock odysseys like 'She's A Superstar' and 'Gravity Grave', few people could have predicted that they'd ever be a singles band. But here they were, some of the best singles of the Nineties. That they weren't arranged in chronological order means that there's almost an element of comic timing in the way that the acid-freak-out of 'All In The Mind' gives way to 'The Drugs Don't Work'.

The album was also used to give a belated release to two songs that didn't make it on to *Urban Hymns.* 'Monaco' and 'This Could Be My Moment' were both demoed at the original Olympic Studio sessions but they were left off the final tracklisting. In the latter case, it might have been because the title sounded like something from the Eurovision Song Contest. That the album didn't do as well as some singles collections probably boiled down to the fact that most of their fans felt they'd already got all the Verve singles they needed on *Urban Hymns.* The timing of the release was also rather strange – not long after Richard's least successful solo album (when it was re-released in 2007 to coincide with The Verve's latest reunion shows, it made a lot more sense).

After *Human Conditions*, Richard went back to his mansion and must have wondered whether anybody cared anymore. But, by now, Sonny was three years old and they'd discovered that Kate was pregnant again. That same year they had a second son, Cassius, named after Mohammed Ali's original name.

Although his critics accused him of becoming soft and complacent since he'd had children, in some ways fatherhood just made him more anxious. As he astutely noted in an interview with America's *National Post*, he didn't feel like he'd "settled down" as the cliché has it. "'Settling down' – those words are from the Walt Disney book of family life," he said. "Because often, it brings more chaos into your life than you can ever imagine. It brings a deeper understanding of yourself and your own failings and the failings of people around you, and also how much you can love something or someone – all those emotions."

As a single, childless man, he'd understandably never worried too much about the future or the state of the world. At that point in your life, few people do. Now, like most parents, he worried almost all the time. When Sonny was first born, he talked about travelling with him to New York and suddenly becoming aware of a million dangers that he'd never noticed before.

"I'd get off a plane and be met by some guy I never saw before," he said to Thomas Beller, "and think, *Who is this guy picking us up in the airport? Is he drunk or on drugs?*" Later on, he said that he'd been prescribed Prozac in the middle of the decade to try and cope with recurring bouts of depression. In the end he had to accept that the only thing which really helped was making music but the period between recording *Human Conditions* and the next album – *Keys To The World* – was the longest he'd gone without recording since he was 19 years old. He carried on writing, coming up with the downbeat 'Break The Night With Colour', but it would be almost three years before he would finish recording it.

After touring the second album, his only live appearance in early 2004 was at the Royal Festival Hall gig of another one of his heroes – David Axelrod. David Axelrod was a Sixties producer, arranger and songwriter with the group Electric Prunes. His career probably acted as a reassuring parable for Richard. Axelrod's solo records were never particularly successful at the time of their release but, years later, his orchestral, beat-heavy tunes were rediscovered by a generation of hip-hop producers such as DJ Shadow and Dr Dre. The Verve had often come on-stage to the Electric Prunes' 'Holy Are You' and Richard was a massive fan.

He was visibly nervous, then, as he walked on to provide a soft, resonant vocal to a version of the same song. On leaving the stage he mouthed the word "genius". He'd never been shy about acknowledging his heroes and, in a way, he lived in an alternative universe where uncommercial artists like Axelrod or Can were just as important as The Rolling Stones, The Beach Boys or The Beatles.

But, as 2004 went on, he watched as his era seemed to pass into history. His old comrades Oasis were now seen as rock dinosaurs, still plodding along with their large hardcore following but rarely winning over any new fans. Coldplay who, Richard once noted, seemed to be influenced by Nick McCabe's big guitar sound, had now turned into a stadium act and by 2005 critics were declaring that a new era of Britpop was starting. Bands like Snow Patrol were about to become massive with exactly the kind of light melancholia that had been the dominating mood on *Human Conditions*. Just as before The Verve started, rock stars were out of fashion. Maybe Richard had been ahead of his time after all?

The pace of cultural change was even quicker than it had been ten years before and to many Richard Ashcroft no longer seemed like an important figure in music. However, John Best astutely remarks that, despite its relatively poor sales, 'History' had inadvertently become a blueprint for "drippy rock music" for the next decade. And, what was more, the people who made that "drippy rock music" knew that they owed him a debt. Coldplay's Chris Martin actually sounded genuinely outraged in one interview about the critical reception that *Human Conditions* received. It was a gesture that Richard appreciated.

"Chris Martin was one of the few of my peers to publicly speak up, especially in England, on my last album and say: 'Look, I think there's moments of greatness on this record. I think people have got it wrong and you don't understand where he's coming from,'" he said in an interview with Jane Stevenson of the *Toronto Sun*.

It would be hard to find two less similar frontmen than Chris Martin and Richard Ashcroft. Coldplay's gift was making epic-sounding music that still had a humble, everyman quality. They had tunes that weren't a million miles from some of The Verve and Oasis's records but without the starriness or the swagger. Nevertheless Chris was still slightly in awe of people like that. He looked up to them and couldn't understand why they didn't always get the respect that their back catalogue said they deserved. He also had a keen sense of loyalty to the bands who'd helped inspire Coldplay. In 2004 he helped Embrace relaunch their career by giving them a single, 'Gravity', which he'd written and then decided that it was more like one of their songs. In 2005, for Richard Ashcroft, he went a step further.

CHAPTER 16

THE KEYS TO THE WORLD

July 2005 was the 20th anniversary of the biggest event music had ever seen – Live Aid. 1.5 billion people had watched the series of concerts at cities around the world. Over 82,000 people attended the concert at Wembley Stadium in London; 99,000 at the JFK Stadium in Philadelphia. Although there had been charity concerts before, there had never been anything quite like it.

By 2005, though, people's attitude towards charity had changed. Compassion fatigue had set in because there were so many different causes clamouring for attention. Also, the whole concept of the rich rock star using their position to try and persuade ordinary people to donate money was often greeted with great cynicism.

In July, then, Bob Geldof announced that the successor to the original Live Aid project – entitled Live 8 – wouldn't be about the rattling of collection tins. It was about raising awareness of the vast amounts of money the Third World had to pay the rich world in interest payments on its debt. How successfully it did this would be a highly controversial issue later; one widely-remarked side-effect was that it dramatically raised awareness of all the bands and artists who played the concert.

Some of the biggest names in music were booked to play the London show: Robbie Williams, Pink Floyd, U2, Paul McCartney and Madonna. By now, Coldplay could count themselves among this number. Their May 2005 album *X&Y* sold over eight million copies, went straight in at number one in 22 countries and would become the best selling album of the year. Richard had met Chris Martin but he didn't really know him. He was surprised when the singer asked if he wanted to meet up and even more surprised when he then, over dinner, asked him to join Coldplay on stage at Live 8 to perform 'Bitter Sweet Symphony'.

He'd never particularly liked hanging out with other members of bands. The Gallaghers were among the only musicians he genuinely got on with. Despite his image he didn't particularly enjoy hanging out with loud-mouthed stars but the Coldplay singer's humility made a big impact. "A lot of rock stars get this bizarre idea that they're outrageously special, but Coldplay are very humble and genuinely sweet," he said in a radio interview.

He joined them for one rehearsal at Crystal Palace in south London and was immediately convinced that it could work. He was impressed that Chris could play the chorus of 'Life's An Ocean' from *A Northern Soul* on the guitar. "Christ," he commented in an interview with TV's Vernon Kaye. "Even I don't know that!" Coldplay were big fans of The Verve and he could see that they were on the same wavelength. "From that one rehearsal I thought we could pull it off," he said. "It felt natural because they'd been through the school of Verve rock!"

Typically his attitude on the day was an understandable mixture of bravado and nervousness. "I'm looking forward to blowing those fuckers off stage," he half-joked of Coldplay. "I'm sat outside a Portakabin smoking a cigarette, drinking a beer, wondering whether Elton and David are going to kidnap me and take me back to Buckinghamshire to sort me out!" he told *The Daily Telegraph's* Craig McLean.

His nervousness was tempered slightly by an appearance from Bob Geldof. "I still felt a bit like an uninvited guest until Bob Geldof put his arm around me before I went on stage and said 'you're my favourite singer in the world'," he told *GQ*.

That feeling lasted until he stepped out on to the stage in front of over 200,000 people and Chris Martin announced him by declaring: "This is probably the best song ever written and here's the best singer in the world, Mr Richard Ashcroft."

"Any human being would be nervous in that position!" he said. "But it's like any live event, whether it's 200 people or two billion, I don't give a fuck. I'm the man for the job!"

Unfortunately, his performance at Live 8 wasn't quite up to his normal stellar standards. He came on with his usual showmanship, holding his boots over his head and clapping them together. But, when he came to sing, his voice sounded a little gruff and tense.

Even he might have felt that Chris Martin had over-sold him slightly. "It was a great moment," he said with admirable honesty in a radio interview with former Inspiral Carpet member Clint Boon, "but when you're losing your voice after five dates and you know you're not going to be the best singer in the world, that makes it a different kettle of fish."

Although he appreciated Chris's compliment, it put him in an awkward position as, for months afterwards, he was asked about it in interviews. It was hard to know what to say.

"I've been around the world now and everybody's asking me about what Chris Martin said about me," he said. It also made it sound like the day was solely about him rather than the cause. In the same interview he complained that he hadn't been given any feedback from the organisers about what happened after Live 8.

"Because Bob Geldof hasn't given me any information about what we did or didn't achieve, I'm just left floundering in a 100 interviews talking about my own ego," he said to Clint. "That whole day was supposedly about giving up ego to do something for countries that are crippled by debt."

As with most big charity concerts, it did seem like the artists performing initially benefited much more than the official recipients. Many of the bands received hostile headlines after their sales shot up while the level of debt relief remained a murky, controversial subject. The world leaders at the G8 summit announced major changes but some people were cynical about how much was ultimately achieved. Shortly after the interview with Clint, though, Richard decided that he needed to find out whether it had all been more than a gigantic marketing stunt.

"It's easy to be cynical," he said to Stephen Trousse of *Uncut* magazine. "I rang up Bob Geldof and said, 'Look Bob, I've not heard anything back since we did that day – what did we achieve?' And the next day I got this pile of A4. *Billions* written off."

For all this, Live 8 did remind the world that Richard Ashcroft was a star and, for the first time since *Alone With Everybody,* there was intense media interest in what he'd do next. "Not since Lazarus came forth has there been a comeback quite as spectacular as that of Richard Ashcroft," *The Guardian's* Alexis Petridis declared. "Four years after his second solo album, *Human Conditions*, flopped, the former Verve frontman eschewed the traditional path – fan club-only gigs, new songs tentatively circulated on the web – in favour of being introduced as 'the best singer in the world' before an audience of two billion."

It also put a lot of pressure on him. The title of the new album – *Keys To The World* – went back to the holiday he had in Rome with Kate after 'Bitter Sweet Symphony' had suddenly turned him into an international star. "I didn't realise how big the band was," he said to Jacqui Swift of *The Sun*, "and I was trapped in a shop by photographers with hundreds of people outside. I thought: 'Wow, I've got the keys to the world but what the hell am I going to do when I get there?'"

That was almost ten years previously, but he was still struggling with the same conflict between his desire to be left alone and his desire to have the whole world listen to his songs. He knew that being a huge star and selling millions of records didn't make him happy but at the same time he was still confused by the reception *Human Conditions* received. Even more than on previous albums, then, *Keys To The World* found him pondering the meaning of life.

"When I was doing this album," he said to Dorian Lynskey in an interview with *The Big Issue*, "I'd get into taxis every night and say, 'So what's it all about?' And it's amazing. Some people would rant for 25 minutes giving me the answer and some people would be like, 'What are you talking about, man?'"

This might have struck a nerve. For the last two albums 'What's it all about?' was the dominant lyrical theme of many of his songs and many critics had responded with variations on, 'What are you talking about, man?'" Richard had the frustrating feeling that he wasn't getting through to people. After *Human Conditions* he felt deeply misunderstood, even by some of those closest to him.

"I was always a freewheeling guy who arrived in London with no shoes and a bin-bag full of clothes," he said to Dorian, "and suddenly I'm supposed to be Mr Rock Star buying everybody a house. I want to get away from Rock Star bullshit."

When he began writing the new record, then, many of the lyrics were his attempt to grapple with the major issues of the day. It was a more outward-looking album than either *Alone With Everybody* or *Human Conditions*. One of his best new songs was sparked off by a comment from Kate's dad Brian. They were talking about religion and Brian asked why people find it so hard to accept that there's no God. "Why not nothing?" he asked rhetorically.

Although Richard's philosophy was a new-age melting pot, which still contained religious elements, he'd been opposed to organised religion since the day his dad died. This feeling had grown after September 11.

"I wrote this song a few years ago when I was feeling completely disillusioned with all the establishments," he said of 'Why Not Nothing?' on his website. "It's a ranting two chord rock 'n' roll tune that's asking why we can't accept that there's no greater power."

Another song, 'Sweet Brother Malcolm' was even more outward looking. "It's about the floral tributes you see when you're driving around," he explained on his website. "Sometimes you ignore them and sometimes you think about the pain involved and the stories behind them."

He seemed better at this kind of thing than he was at the vague generalities that had appeared on many of his records. Even love songs like 'Cry Till The Morning' and 'Why Do Lovers?' had a harder edge to them than similar songs on his previous solo albums. In his track-by-track commentary he said that the latter track was about a couple's relationship being tested, and perhaps strengthened, by hard times.

But this intimate, personal approach didn't extend to the recording of the album. He'd still got a big advance to spend and the sessions for *Keys To The World* would be as lavish as ever. To begin with, he went into Terry Britten's studio State Of The Ark. Terry was a producer and songwriter who'd written 'Devil Woman' for Cliff Richard and co-written 'What's Love Got To Do With It?' among other huge hits. His studio had a mixture of vintage, analogue equipment and modern technology. Once again Richard would have the money, the time and the equipment to do absolutely anything he wanted.

So on the title track, for example, he would throw in a looped female vocal that sounded like it belonged on a Nineties dance record and then on another track, 'Break The Night With Colour', there would be twangy harpsichord which dragged things back towards the 18th Century. However, there were some signs that he'd listened to the criticisms of *Human Conditions*. That record was drenched in syrupy strings but on *Keys To The World*, Richard dispensed with the services of Wil Malone for the first time since 'History'.

This time Julian Kershaw of the London Metropolitan Orchestra was asked to provide an arrangement. The London Metropolitan Orchestra were best known for their work providing scores for film and TV. Their main role was to provide an atmosphere rather than carry a song in the way that Richard's orchestral elements had in the past.

Another ghost of the past was laid to rest with 'Music Is Power'. Ten years after he wrote, or at least put together 'Bitter Sweet Symphony', he at last had the confidence to borrow a bit of somebody else's tune again. The track contained a sample from a song written by Curtis Mayfield and played by soul artist Walter Jackson. It came about on a holiday Richard took in the south of France. He was listening to a tape somebody had made him with Walter Jackson's *It's All Over* on it and he started singing his own lyrics over the top. By the time he'd got home, he couldn't resist rushing into the studio and turning it into a new song.

Fortunately the riff isn't quite as central to the music as 'Bitter Sweet Symphony's sample was, though, and Richard made sure to deal with the legal issues in advance: "I just made damn sure that we got the publishing all sorted out this time!" he said.

When the album *Keys To The World* arrived, it surprised many people. The opening track 'Why Not Nothing?' wasn't another pleasantly low-key ballad. Beginning with an impassioned blast of brass and guitars, it made it quite clear that he didn't want to make background music. When his vocal came in it was unlike anything on his previous records, a hoarse rant more reminiscent of Bob Dylan than the more soulful style he'd been using recently. It was his best song for a long time and all the better because it was such a departure.

What makes it so good is the combination between the aggression and simplicity of the concept and the exuberance of the brass. It could be seen as an angry song with a happy vibe or a happy song with angry lyrics.

The second track, 'Music Is Power', was more similar to the songs on *Human Conditions*. It had that same gospel feel with a rhythm that skips along incongruously beneath a vocal that is slightly more downbeat than either the brassy music or the lyric. There were strings, too, but they weren't quite as high up in the mix as they'd been in the past.

The third track, 'Break The Night With Colour', saw him veering decisively back towards the middle of the road again. The harpsichord gave it a classic, simple sound and his voice alternated between a rough, serious growl on the verses and a soulful 'oooh' on the chorus. It was mid-tempo and mid-everything else, too: another in a long series of nice tunes with all their edges knocked off in the studio. The only real grit to it is the mournful complaint about "fools" who don't understand him. Presumably this meant either the critics who dismissed *Human Conditions* or the people who had laughed at his various grandiose statements over the years. Like so many of his songs, it takes his characteristic attitude of glum optimism: things are pretty bad now but they could be better in the future if we try.

As so often, though, it seemed like he was almost too concerned with making everything perfect. The album's big ballad, 'Words Just Get In The Way', had a beautiful melody but, like many of his previous ballads, it was surrounded by too much extraneous accompaniment. It starts with a raw vocal and delicate keyboard but then the guitars come in, then strings, and then a French Horn. It's not quite so syrupy as similar tracks on *Alone With Everybody* but it might have benefited from a less grandiose performance.

Luckily the title track stirs things up again. Built around a dancey vocal loop from ex-Zero 7 collaborator Yvonne John-Lewis, it's catchy and full of an energy that's missing from most of his solo output. In his desire to be make 'classic' songs, it occasionally seemed like he'd forgotten that it was the 21st century. 'Keys To The World' was a kind of wake-up call. His staccato, megaphone vocal towards the end even comes close to rap – another big departure.

Fittingly, considering he'd now got the London Metropolitan Orchestra involved, 'Sweet Brother Malcolm' sounds like it should be on the soundtrack of some heartstring-tugging ITV drama. Despite this, the emotion behind the song is easier to relate to for not being about the problems of a wealthy pop star. Not directly, anyway. When he talks about the press descending on the town after the accident, it's not hard to see some parallels. It's not quite 'The Drugs Don't Work' but it has a welcome rawness about it.

The next track, 'Cry Til The Morning', is a pretty extraordinary song in its own way. It's the kind of thing John Lennon might have written in his later days. It's a love song but one which seems to be powered by the sadness prior to a relationship rather than the relationship itself. Ironically, it's reminiscent of something Jason Pierce of Spiritualized might have written after the break-up of his relationship with Kate Radley. It starts with simple, slightly eerie keyboard and then a raw, gruff vocal. But instead of slathering on the plush strings, they're kept well in the background and some fuzzy, distorted guitar comes in instead.

'Why Do Lovers?' starts out with an even more understated keyboard riff. His vocal on the track is barely recognisable in places from the confident, bold voice of 'Bitter Sweet Symphony'. It's much gruffer, tormented, almost. Unfortunately, although you can make out the basis of a powerful song, this time the strings are let off the leash and they absolutely swarm across the track, blotting out the impact of his highly emotional performance.

The next track, 'Simple Song', was one of those he'd written way back in 1996. He even recorded a version of it with Youth at the initial sessions for what would later become *Urban Hymns*. It uses the strings much more effectively, filling in the gaps between his vocal with little flourishes or attacking in unison with a fantastically catchy piano and guitar riff.

Tunes like 'Why Not Nothing?' and 'Keys To The World' almost imagine an alternative solo career for Richard Ashcroft, where he hadn't spent ten years trying to replicate the success of 'The Drugs Don't Work' but gone for a more energetic, high-tempo sound.

The title of the last track, 'World Keeps Turning', is the kind of thing you might imagine a Richard Ashcroft random song-title generator would come up with. The song itself wasn't bad at all. It's very Dylan in the rasping vocal but he's by no means hitting the listener over the head with the song's message. There's a looseness to it as though at last he's let go of the idea that every song he writes has to change the world. Because of that, it's a fine ending to what is, probably, Richard's best solo album.

His big 'comeback' single, 'Break The Night With Colour', was released on January 9, 2006. It managed his usual trick of sounding musically low-key and downbeat while the slightly odd lyric, a jumble sale of mixed metaphors, was as grandiose as ever. The accompanying video had him banged up in prison. Initially he's sitting glumly plonking away at the piano, the sound echoing down empty corridors, then he plays with a ball for a bit before, eventually, the warders let him out. Even then he doesn't look particularly pleased, which might have been a statement of sorts. Was he saying that his recent life had been like being in prison? Or just that he'd run out of video concepts that involved filming him walking down the street?

'Break The Night With Colour' wasn't his best song, the lyrics let it down but the central melody was very strong and, with his new higher profile, it went straight in at number three in the UK charts. Once again, there was a story for the media to tell.

"Every time you do a record it's always 'he's back' or 'he's back on form'", Richard complained to Vernon Kaye. "Really, you never go away. That's that culture we're living in at the moment. Everything has to have a label. Everything has to be put in a chicken nugget that they think we'll understand."

Not long after the release of the single, he supported Coldplay on their North American tour. It was a chance to reintroduce himself to fans who might vaguely remember 'Bitter Sweet Symphony' but who would have had little exposure to him since.

"If you're fool enough to put me on before you, do it!" he laughed. Once again, just as The Verve had arrived with the tide of shoe-gazing and then made their biggest inroads in the Britpop era, it almost seemed like he was part of some kind of a 'scene' again. Only this time it was a return to widescreen, wistful epics of mild melancholia. It wasn't cool in the way that shoe-gazing and Britpop had been at their inception but at least it gave him an audience and airplay. He felt like things had moved his way slightly. When *Human Conditions* came out he'd complained that "everyone was pretending they were all at CBGB's in 1977 or something."

Keys To The World was released on January 23, 2006, and went platinum, reaching number two, just behind the massively popular Arctic Monkeys. It ultimately sold far more copies than *Human*

Conditions. He was then able to announce his biggest UK tour for years, ending up by playing three nights at London's Brixton Academy. It was a major comeback and when he did interviews around the release, he was in rightly confident mood. "Anyone who says you ain't done anything better than *Urban Hymns* can fuck off or wait around for a head–butt," he growled.

Initially, the only downside was the lack of interest outside the UK. *Break The Night With Colour* got considerable airplay at home but in the US, radio still wasn't interested and Richard, once again, blamed the fact that he no longer had his old 'trade name' The Verve. Perhaps he started to wonder whether he would be better off with his old compadres?

The second single off the album was 'Music Is Power' and maybe it wasn't the best choice. It was more like the disappointing 'Money To Burn' than anything else on the record and, although it was far superior to that song, it wasn't one of the album's best moments. The video, too, didn't work as well as it might. Once again it showed him walking along directly towards the camera. The only slight twist, if you could call it that, was that he was walking along a corridor rather than a street. Oh, and as with 'Money To Burn', when he bumped into somebody, he immediately apologised.

The song peaked at number 20 in the UK charts and then immediately plummeted, which wasn't quite part of the plan. Nevertheless, he was still able to announce the biggest solo date of his career, a homecoming gig of sorts at Manchester's Old Trafford Cricket Ground on June 17. "I just want to do a big gig in the north west," he told local paper the *Bolton News*. "Manchester's buzzing at the moment like it always has, and I've got a massive connection with the city obviously, so there were other reasons for playing Old Trafford than because you can pack 30,000 people into here. It goes a lot deeper than that."

Originally he'd wanted to perform at Wigan Athletic but when he couldn't get permission, the cricket ground was the next best thing. He dreamed of giving local kids the impetus to go and create something themselves in the same way that he'd been inspired.

"I'm expecting it to be very emotional," he said to the *South Manchester Reporter*. "I know for a fact there were people inspired when The Verve played Haigh Hall in Wigan and I want this to inspire people to make it happen for themselves. Like I was when I saw the Roses."

With Razorlight and The Feeling supporting, the gig sold out. Razorlight, in particular, was a band that had rapidly become big in the last couple of years with a frontman, Johnny Borrell, whose style surely owed a great deal to Richard Ashcroft. They were managed by Roger Morton, who'd famously interviewed Richard for *NME* all those years ago, and Roger says that the similarity between the two stars was one of the things that made him think Razorlight might go places.

"When I first met Johnny I thought about that quite a lot," he says. "Obviously musically they're very different but in terms of persona you have some of the same ingredients. I thought Johnny had some of Richard in him and some of Nick McCabe as well. It was one of the things that made me believe in Johnny and Razorlight because I'd seen what had happened with The Verve."

The performance should have been the culmination of one of the best fortnight's of Richard's solo career but instead it turned out to be one of the worst. On June 11, he played at the Isle Of Wight and seemed more fired up than ever. As well as shouting, "Bring the boys home, Tony. Bring them home!" and warning everybody not to vote for Cameron or Blair because they're "fucking liars," some fans thought that he seemed to have more personal issues.

"This next song is for anyone who's thinking of killing themselves," he said before 'Break The Night With Colour'", "This song is for you. I'm so fucking glad you're here today."

"He's clearly gone through something wrenching recently," said *The Independent* at the time. It was one of his most powerful performances, particularly an acoustic version of 'The Drugs Don't Work' where his voice was almost drowned out by the crowd; however, fans were concerned about what he'd just said.

The Old Trafford gig was less than a week later and once again he was furiously fired up. Arriving on stage to Primal Scream's 'Come Together' and bellowing "Come on Manchester!" there was no indication that he was having problems. 'Music Is Power' was changed to 'Rooney Is Power' in homage to Manchester United's new star striker and, in a further bit of currying favour, he told his fans they were the best crowd he'd ever had. It was a feeling that was reciprocated. By now when he played live he had an enviable set list. The best songs of his solo career combined with tracks from The Verve demonstrated, once again, what a fine songwriter he was.

'Lucky Man' was introduced as "one of the greatest songs I ever wrote", and 'Bitter Sweet Symphony' and 'The Drugs Don't Work' were as triumphant as they were at the Isle Of Wight. The encore even saw a surprise appearance from DJ Shadow to perform their brilliant 'Lonely Soul' collaboration from UNKLE's *Psyence Fiction* album.

Roger Morton met Richard backstage at Old Trafford for the first time since their 1992 interview and at that point he seemed fine, almost euphoric. "I bumped into him after he came off-stage when he was in the toilets and we had a little chat," Roger says, "and I said, 'Do you remember me from all those years ago when we did that first interview?' and he said he did, which was sweet."

But two days later he was arrested at Bridge Centre Youth Club in Chippenham in Wiltshire, near where Kate's parents live. Apparently drunk, he'd walked past the club, looked in to see the 60 or so kids and felt an overwhelming desire to help them.

There were no musical instruments on display and he thought this was just wrong. He said afterwards that he suddenly imagined the kind of great things that could happen if they just had guitars and a small, home recording studio.

"He was … close to tears at one point," the BBC reported one eyewitness as saying. "He kept saying he wanted to work with kids, that he wanted to do 'good things.' He wasn't aggressive, in fact he was quite charming and friendly. He kept hugging some staff and kids."

Despite this he was in an alarming state. "He looked like a tramp," they continued. "He was dishevelled and unshaven with filthy clothes and there was saliva caked around his mouth … although he wasn't slurring his words. One of the staff said: 'You're the spitting image of Richard Ashcroft,' and he said, 'That's because I am.'"

After he refused to leave, slumping on a sofa, the police were called. They, too, tried to reason with him but he ended up being taken into custody for a couple of hours and fined £80. Richard's record label refused to comment but the singer realised what he'd done, and spoke very honestly to the media. "I completely understand the fuss," he said. "It doesn't matter who you are, you can't just walk in off the street. It was stupid of me. And the police turned up. It was ridiculous."

In his defence, there is something quite endearing about the fact that, at his most vulnerable, with his inhibitions removed, his first thought was that he should volunteer to help out at a youth club. He'd always talked about his feeling that there weren't enough opportunities for young people.

"My message would be – give a kid a guitar not an ASBO," he'd said a couple of years previously to *The Mirror*. "Give him space to express himself. Over the next few years that's what I want to do – wake people up to the talent that exists on working class estates in Glasgow, Manchester, Liverpool, the North East right down to Cornwall."

It was a recurring theme in his interviews. He remembered how hard it had been for kids to express themselves when he was growing up in Wigan. Around the time of the Old Trafford gig, he was thinking about the issue seriously and, from what he said when he spoke to *The Bolton News* immediately prior to that, it was clear what was on his mind when he walked past the youth club.

"If you give a kid a paintbrush and some paints or a brick, you'd be surprised that he'll pick the paintbrush up every time and start creating," he told reporter Kat Dibbits. "We're in a different age now and the government should give money to deprived areas to give them a computer and a small desk and a way into making music."

He also hinted that he sometimes felt making music on its own wasn't enough to fulfill him. "I want to use the position I'm in to do some good on this planet," he said, "because I've squandered a lot of time."

After this incident, there was obviously a lot of concern about his state of mind. He did say that he'd tried taking Prozac to deal with his depression but that it hadn't helped. "If I lived in LA, I'd be seeing someone three times a day, every day," he said. "But I'm a northern Englishman dealing with his shit in his own way." Part of the problem seemed to go back to the same question that he'd been asking taxi drivers while making *Keys To The World*. He still wanted to know what it was all about.

When he was doing press for the *Alone With Everybody* album, people noticed that Richard had started wearing a crucifix. He often talked about Jesus and had a kind of vague spirituality that was hard to define but seemed to be a personalised version of Anglicanism. His main gripe with religion was the things that were done in its name, rather than the central premise.

"With so many songs mentioning God, is it safe to assume you're a religious man," *VH1* once asked him. "No, not really," he replied. "It's safe to assume that I believe a man named Jesus lived on this planet. It's safe to assume that in my kids' eyes, my wife's eyes, and a cup of tea, I feel something that resembles a higher power. I still consider myself a seeker and a fan of Charles Darwin and William Blake. But, I'm also obsessed with the concept of a glass confessional box so the priest won't abuse you."

Still, he was brought up a Christian and some of that seems to have stayed with him despite his understandable loss of faith when his dad died. He was confirmed purely, he said, because he wanted "a piece of jewellery" – a chain with his name on – but it seems like the influence of his Sunday School teachers never quite left him. When his stepdad introduced him to the beliefs of the Rosicrucians at 14, he seemed to mix that with a New Testament belief in an afterlife and something beyond the physical world.

The attraction of the Rosicrucian order was that they taught that strength and wisdom came from within. This appealed to Richard's instinctive dislike of being told what to do and his feeling that he was capable of great things. "Discover how extraordinary you really are," the order enticingly promises. As a teenager, he took from the order an absolute belief that he was the master of his own destiny and that practical problems simply didn't matter all that much. There was something more important in the universe.

This feeling strengthened when he became a musician. He felt that the process of creating music involved tapping into the spirit world. This came across in a desire to make a kind of modern day "devotional music". Songs like 'Sonnet', he believed, were close to gospel.

"If you heard a choir sing that, you wouldn't argue with it," he said to Jay Babcock of *Mean Machine*. It was also important that so many of his heroes, such as Al Green, invoked God. He'd always admired the way that black American soul artists could express their spiritual beliefs in a way that white British artists couldn't, at least not without being ridiculed by the press.

It was part of a more general feeling he had that the middle-class English establishment tried to crush anybody who expressed their emotions without the veil of irony. Right back at the beginning of his career, he invoked Jimi Hendrix's 'Voodoo Chile', complaining in *Melody Maker* that, "Bands couldn't say anything like, 'I'm a voodoo chile', today – there'd be jokes in *Melody Maker* for the rest of the year if they did. But you should be able to say what you want – it's your space, use it."

These were prophetic words. Almost every time he came to promote a record he seemed to say things that would incite controversy or ridicule. He didn't understand why, say, Lee 'Scratch' Perry could be acclaimed despite – or because of – his infamous eccentricity or why Al Green and Johnny Cash could sing about God without anybody laughing at them. In his early life, however, his search for an alternative way of life perhaps involved consuming acid.

The drugs were initially linked directly to the music he was listening to. He took them, he told *Guardian* journalist Sylvia Patterson "to hear music on 50,000 different levels – I wanted to be blown apart" and then "to see solid objects morph into things that my mind wanted them to be."

But by the time he was 20, he was already starting to feel the ill-effects. "Anyone who preaches about the positive aspect of any drugs, it's just boring," he told journalist Thomas Beller. "I think it's quite horrifying the amount of people who have burnt out and lost their mind, the acid casualties. The same is true of cocaine, just the amount of empty promising, the amount of bullshit."

But there remained perhaps a spiritual void because he couldn't find any religion or philosophy that made sense. This comes across quite movingly in 'Buy It In Bottles'. He would like to be a believer but, as 'Why Not Nothing?' also said, religion has done too much harm.

"Jesus Christ for the past 2,000 years has been used and abused by this ragtag bunch of power-hungry people," he said to Tom Lanham. "And now you've got a lot of people trying to say that they've seen the light, that their God is literally all our God, that the president's

God is my God. And that is freakish beyond belief."

Despite this, he's often spoken about his admiration for Jesus. Slightly more controversially, at the beginning of 2006, he even identified himself with Jesus. "I love the man, I feel like him," he said in *NME* of Jesus. "There's only Richard Ashcroft and Liam Gallagher who know what it feels like. We're the only ones who know how many people we've touched and how powerful that is, I feel like I'm on a one-man mission. I'm here to use my tools and my gift to take them to a higher level."

It was the same kind of hyperbole that he'd come out with throughout his career and the result was the same – a storm of ridicule. Later he complained that the way his rants were edited down made it appear that he was saying something more controversial than he really was.

"I'd just like to clear up all this Jesus business," he said at a performance for Radio Two. "I don't think I'm Jesus Christ, what I was trying to say is that we should all be looking to him for inspiration in life – it just came out wrong. But you try answering questions when you're having your picture taken for *NME* at six o'clock on a Monday morning, y'know?" That sounded like a perfectly reasonable defence and, besides, he wouldn't be the first rock star to object to the way a quote of his had been printed. Also, if he was wearing any shoes, you perhaps had to walk a mile in them to see the situation through his eyes.

But introspection was as much a part of his character and his music as his previous hell-raising. It constantly drove him to better himself but at times it made him wonder if making music was enough.

CHAPTER 17

THE BIG THAW

After coming back with a bang, the *Keys To The World* campaign didn't take long to fizzle out. Curiously the next single was 'Words Just Get In The Way', not one of the stand-out tracks from the album. It got little airplay, peaked at number 40 in the UK chart and then disappeared. It seemed like he had a hardcore of fans who were still loyal but that few other people remained interested after the post-Live 8 splash.

"An evening with one of his albums is a little bit like being nine and winning the chance to have dinner with your hero," said Peter Paphides in a review of *Keys To The World* for *The Times*. "The entire enterprise is pointless if you don't already believe they are amazing."

The album's best song 'Why Not Nothing?' was released in a limited edition double A-side with 'Sweet Brother Malcolm', but by then the spotlight had drifted away from him. At the same time, various other plans had come to nothing. He'd talked about re-recording 'C'Mon People' as 'C'Mon England' for England's World Cup Football campaign but, perhaps fortunately, that didn't happen. He wanted to work with DJ Shadow on a full album but this never materialised.

After that he talked enthusiastically about an album of covers. For most artists this would mean covering other people's songs, perhaps as a homage to artists they loved. Naturally, Richard meant he wanted other people to cover *his* songs!

"Dolly Parton doing 'The Drugs Don't Work' would be an incredible thing," he said. "She's one of the greatest singers in the world and it's one of the best songs ever written." At the time he'd also become a fan of Johnny Cash. He had ambitions of working with Rick Rubin – Cash's legendary producer. He said that Rick thought he was an "an arrogant Northern English guy". But, with typical confidence, he said, "I'll persuade him."

To date that hasn't happened either, unfortunately. By the end of 2006, he was pretty much back where he'd been before 'Live 8'. Although *Keys To The World* was a success compared with *Human Conditions*, it hadn't put him back up where he'd been with The Verve. The brand-name 'Richard Ashcroft' was still basically a niche concern, to use the record biz parlance. There was one thing everybody knew wouldn't happen though. As Richard said when asked in 2005 if there was any chance of a reunion of The Verve. "There's more chance of getting all four Beatles on stage together!"

But maybe the fact that *Keys To The World* had done better than the last two solo albums made the reunion that bit more likely? It meant that he didn't have quite so much to prove. He was still a star and he could still sell-out big shows on his own. Right back in 1996 he'd said when he supported Oasis at Madison Square Garden that he didn't like being solo. Although his enormous self-belief meant that he found the compromise of life in a band difficult, he also liked the security of having other musicians around him. He was also conscious that his greatest talent lay in his ability to get the best out of others and to put different ideas together.

And in a sense The Verve remained unfinished business. For all their great songs, they hadn't produced an album where they were all consistently pulling together since *A Storm In Heaven*. The conflicts within the band had produced some amazingly productive creative tension but they'd also created a situation where it almost seemed like there were two Verves – Richard Ashcroft's version and the band's.

By the end of 2006, it was probably the case that all four members might have welcomed a reunion. Richard and Peter had remained together through everything and they were both aware that it might be hard to sell another Richard Ashcroft album. They could hardly hope for another Live 8 or another endorsement from whoever happened to be flavour of the month.

Nick McCabe was just as obsessed with music as Richard and yet he'd hardly produced anything of note since the jam sessions that rounded off *Urban Hymns*, while Si Jones' band The Shining, had long since broken up. Maybe the problem was that they were all too proud to be the first one to call? As John Best observed, they'd never been all that good at communicating with each other.

But there were other wider reasons why The Verve reforming was becoming more likely. During the first few years of the 21st Century, one after another great and not so great band was getting back together. Even those who'd split citing the most irreconcilable of differences were now back doing it, "for the music". When the remaining members of The Beatles (and John Lennon in virtual form) got together for 'Free As A Bird' in 1995, it seemed to open the floodgates.

Indie acts who hadn't had a hit for years, like Shed 7, were joined by those, like Led Zeppelin, who had sworn that deceased members could never be replaced. A healthy live scene meant that bands who wouldn't necessarily sell a lot of records could easily draw big crowds to their gigs. Nostalgia was big business and many bands' reputations had grown while they were away. They could double their fanbase. As well as original fans, there was a new generation who'd heard older brothers' or sisters' records but who'd been too young to attend the original gigs.

On purely financial grounds, it must have been difficult for the stars of the past to resist getting back together. Nor should that necessarily be something to recoil from. As Richard so often observed, bands were brands and it was a rare solo career that commanded the fees of a classic pop group. And it wasn't just the band members who had a stake. There were all the other people, the managers, roadies and record label employees, who'd earned a good living. They would all stand to profit if the gravy train started rumbling again.

But, despite this, there were more than just financial concerns going on in the rash of reunions. Many musicians who'd left school early to form a band literally weren't able to do anything else. If music's all you've known and you've only known success with one particular group of people, then why not get back together? After a few years the arguments that might have seemed so bitter and intractable suddenly seem silly and laughable. The good times shine more brightly in the memory than the bad times and, anyway, one tour on your own terms seems like a lot less pressure than a major record deal stretching across numerous years, tours and albums into the future. As Richard once said, most musicians get into bands for the freedom and then a couple of years down the line they know exactly where they're going to be and what they're going to be doing in six months time.

All of these considerations might have played a part when The Verve announced they were getting back together. Or maybe it was just that, as in 1996, they all recognised they still had unfinished business.

"What is the likelihood of a Verve reunion at some point down the line?" *VH1* once asked Richard Ashcroft. "No likelihood," he replied. "Life's too short. When I was recording my first solo album, a mixture of fear in becoming a solo artist and a sense of unfinished business led me to think, 'Let's give Nick a ring and get this going and call it The Verve.' I can't do that again. That was Spinal Tap enough."

The thing about Spinal Tap, though, is that it's uncannily accurate about the lives of many rock bands. In retrospect, it almost seems as though, with Richard's constant assertions that he wouldn't reform the band, that even he knew he was protesting too much. He even, in a funny kind of way, guessed the exact year of the reunion. "Everyone's expecting me to die out like some classic lead singer of a successful rock band," he said to *Planet Rock*. "Or perhaps cry out for a reunion in five years time. It's not going to happen."

That was in 2002. In 2007, Peter Salisbury was working in his drum shop in Stockport when he got a call from Richard. Pete then called Nick and said: "Are you sitting down? Richard wants to put the band back together."

After all those years, it seemed like it was as easy as that. For friends of the band, it was almost like hearing an estranged couple, who've been slagging each over off for years, suddenly announce that they're an item again. It wasn't totally unexpected but it still came as a shock. And a very pleasant one at that.

"Dave Halliwell rang me," says Brian Cannon, "and he said, 'You're not going to fucking believe this Brian.' I said 'What?' He said 'The Verve are getting back together.' You know what my instant reaction was? 'Fuck off!'"

Later on, they admitted that it hadn't been quite as easy as they'd first suggested. Richard spent three hours on the phone with Nick discussing everything that had happened and then Nick phoned Si Jones. But what this meant was, when they went into the studio, they were able to forget about everything that had gone on between them and just concentrate on the music.

Their first meeting was at Terry Britten's State Of The Ark Studios in Richmond. "We all decided," Richard Ashcroft told *NME*, "that rather than meeting for a cup of coffee or a beer or whatever, we should meet in a studio where we can do what we do. Straight away."

Simon Jones was the last person to arrive and within a mere 20 minutes of him walking through the door, they began recording together again for the first time in 11 years. In an interview with *NME* a couple of months later, Nick McCabe said: "Just the social aspect would've been enough for me, just for me to be in a room with these three people again."

This was pretty incredible considering the harsh things that had been said in the past. But then again any friendship that had started as long ago as The Verve's would have been through a few ups and downs. The reality was that none of them, not even Richard, had managed to make as good music alone as they had together.

To begin with they kept the news that they were back a closely guarded secret. "If they hadn't been happy with it, they would have all gone their different ways and nobody would have known," Jazz Summers, now their manager again, told *Mojo*. "That was the reason that we kept it quiet."

"I think me and Si sort of arrived at the same point, mentally really," Nick said in an *NME* interview with Hamish McBain. "We had quite a long time being angry about it, and then once you've sort of resolved a lot of things in your own mind about it, you kind of realise that it wasn't such a big deal in the first place."

They made an official announcement that they were back in June 2007. At the same time, they also announced their first live shows for nine years, a six date tour with two dates each in Glasgow, Blackpool and London. Then the results of that first session were released as a free download with *NME*.com. Starting from the moment they switched the tape recorder on, it caught them in a middle of a long jam with a shimmer of guitar in the background, a rolling, *A Storm In Heaven*-style groove and a keening vocal from Richard. As the tune goes on, more parts are added until the song burns out just as nonchalantly as it started. It was a sign that they still had the same insouciant confidence that they'd always had. Not many bands would be happy to let fans listen to rough, unmastered demos, let alone the first fruits of a jam session before they'd even been formed into a real song.

"This is what you would have heard had you been in the room with us, and you, my friends, get to hear it. Gratis," said Nick on his blog. "Make of that what you will."

The fact that they left the recording so rough, with no attempt to edit it or add an intro, put slightly less pressure on the release. The way the tape starts in the middle of a jam makes the point that this is just a work-in-progress. It was a way of telling the world what The Verve was – not a Richard Ashcroft project but four equal musicians in a room. It was also a way of answering the sceptics who felt that the main motivation for the comeback was money.

"I was very surprised when they got back together," says BJ Cole. "It just felt like it was financially expedient to me, but then those sort of things always do. When people have such a fundamental difference of opinion, when they've known each other all their lives, it's very hard to mend that sort of thing. It's common sense – if people who've known each other from school have disagreements in that way it's very hard to put it back together again."

This was a widely held belief. "I did find that bizarre when they announced that they were getting back together," says website host and fan Ajay Sharma. "It seemed very strange that they would work together again. I mean, I knew they would because everybody gets back together eventually. I'm not so surprised. I heard some of the first live shows, and some of the new songs sound great, so I'm looking forward to seeing them. I like what they're trying to do. I like the fact that they're trying to go back to the old Verve and not just a long version of 'Sonnet' or something like that."

The Sun reported that they'd been offered £20 million to get back together but they scoffed at this idea and vehemently denied any accusations of cashing in. "We haven't had a bean," Simon Jones said. The whole band were adamant that they were doing it for the love of music and the demo, named *The Thaw Sessions*, suggested they might have been telling the truth. While, in its raw, unedited form, it wasn't comparable with anything they'd put on their records, it did radiate the sheer joy of playing together. It might have confused those who only knew them from the singles off *Urban Hymns* but older fans were delighted.

Ex-*NME* journalist and early Verve fan John Mulvey commented on the *Uncut* magazine website that, "listening to it for the second time right now, I'm reminded of a bunch of very early shows I saw the band play, when Nick McCabe's levitating, ambulatory guitar lines seemed to goad Ashcroft into ever more cosmic behaviour."

After the success of that first day back together, they just carried on going and, during their next session at State Of The Ark, they came up with *25* tunes in five days. "The sessions have been pretty amazing," Simon Jones announced just a couple of months later on his MySpace blog. "We certainly have an embarrassment of riches where material is concerned! We will need to do a lot of listening over the next few months before we reconvene in the New Year to pull it all together! Plenty of hour long jams! And killer choons! We just need to get the balance right."

Several new song titles were announced, too. 'Sit And Wonder' – apparently edited down from a long jam; 'Mona Lisa' – described as a more straightforward song that could have been on a Richard Ashcroft album; 'Judas' – a full-on jam with Nick's guitar high in the mix; and 'Rather Be' which Simon Jones said was, "a very vocally led song with lots of intertwining vocals and a string line looping around three chords all the way through … it's just a case of getting a balance between Richard's songs and the more jam-based songs," he said, "if we can get the balance right, then it's gonna be a spectacular record."

There was also a track named 'Appalachian Springs' – presumably in homage to American classical composer Aaron Copland's *Appalachian Spring*. Richard had often said that he was a fan of Copland, particularly of the way that he weaved a thread of folk music through his compositions. It was a similar magpie approach to genres that he liked to think he used in rock music.

After the recording sessions, they returned to a rehearsal studio up north and began practising for the forthcoming tour. "Gotta say," Si Jones reported on his MySpace blog, "twas the greatest few days playin' old tunes!" He even opened the floor to fans to suggest which songs they wanted to hear. Eventually the first gig at Glasgow in November 2007 would feature a setlist that covered the whole of

The Verve's history – 17 tracks – from 'All In The Mind' to new songs like 'Sit And Wonder'.

Before that, though, their first public appearance as The Verve since their break-up was at October's Q Awards, where they won a special 'Classic Album' award for *Urban Hymns*. The relaxed, cheerful looking band went on-stage and Richard made a point of thanking Ian Brown for The Stone Roses.

"This album wouldn't have been made if I hadn't gone to see the Stone Roses that night [in Warrington]," he said. Simon Jones then thanked the bands' wives and children. This alone made the point of how much time had passed since they were last together, as most of the children hadn't even been born when *Urban Hymns* was released.

For Miles Leonard, now the boss of their record label Parlophone, it was an emotional moment. He hadn't worked with them as The Verve since the beginning of the Nineties. "It was incredible when I met up with them all at the *Q Awards* just to see all of them sat round the table," he said. "It was a really special moment."

That first gig in nine years would be less than a month later at Glasgow Academy. The tickets for the relatively small venues had sold out in less than 20 minutes but most people who attended must have had some feeling of apprehension. There's a long history of bands reforming and comprehensively trashing their reputation. With The Verve, things seemed to be different. The reports that came back from Glasgow Academy bordered on the ecstatic. As Richard took his shoes off before he went on-stage and tossed them to one side, just as he always had, it was as though they'd never been away.

"With one single familiar gesture – Ashcroft's customary cry of 'Come on!' and an index finger jabbing at Nick McCabe, the guitarist, the preceding eight years were eradicated instantly," Peter Paphides of *The Times* wrote.

"For those who've seen Ashcroft solo, tonight is a shock of the best kind," said Anthony Thornton in *NME*. "Gone is the dead-behind-the-eyes wannabe MOR soul-singer. The indie messiah in a grandad shirt stalks the stage confidently frying thousands of minds."

Equally, most people who saw them reported, with some surprise, that the band genuinely seemed to be getting on well. Playing live was always the part of the job that they liked most and, whether or not they were at each other's throats offstage, so far the reunion was clearly working. New track 'Sit And Wonder' was particularly encouraging. Built over a huge, rolling bass groove it combined the urgency of their more song-based efforts with the fluidity and power of their jams. "Someone's going to shit themselves at Radio One when they hear that," Richard said at Blackpool.

"It was amazing to see them when I went on the tour and to recognise that they were playing just as they were at their best," says Miles Leonard. "To see Nick come off and say how much he loved it and how much he'd enjoyed playing again was almost a first. He's just an incredible guitarist. The others had been in other bands or solo but Nick went into the wilderness so it was great to see him back on stage."

The first six shows saw them playing to the real hardcore of their fans: the people who'd been waiting for this for years and who loved old songs like 'All In The Mind' as much as 'The Drugs Don't Work'. Even in a more cynical London, the crowd reaction was ecstatic. They weren't there just to rehash the hits. Nick McCabe made clear everybody realised that by attacking 'Bitter Sweet Symphony' with swathes of exhilarating, distorted guitar.

"If there is a change, it's a good one," John Mulvey wrote for *Uncut*. "The Verve's reunion is necessarily predicated on the return of McCabe and, consequently, the band's silvery, psychedelic side is in the ascendant tonight."

And, critics reported cautiously, they still seemed to be comfortable on stage together. "When McCabe isn't turning his back to the audience, bending double over his guitar to wring some deafening washes out of it, he's always glancing at Ashcroft," Kitty Empire reported in *The Observer*. "Jones, meanwhile, charges around like a kid on too many E-numbers, mouthing Ashcroft's words. This does not seem like an icy standoff, endured solely for the money."

A different test would come when they announced the second leg of the tour, playing arena dates across the country. This time they did drop some of the earlier tunes in favour of material from *Urban Hymns* but some critics weren't quite so impressed. The Nottingham show suffered technical problems and dodgy sound. Then at the 02

Arena, Nick got cramp during 'Rolling People' and had to leave the stage temporarily. The biggest news was that Richard had chopped off the famous rock star hair and dyed it blonde.

Overall, the reunion had been a huge success on one level. They'd proved that the band – and indeed the 'brand' – was still a massive commercial draw if nothing else. The next step was to take the various jams they'd put together and create a new album out of them.

While the third coming of The Verve started with a blaze of optimism, the music scene in 2008 was very different than it had been in 1997. The very idea of an album had come under threat from new technology. Most people didn't listen to albums in the way that they had in the past, as a cohesive whole. They listened to them chopped up into their component parts on an iPod.

At the same time, the idea of actually paying for an album was under even more threat. Record labels seemed almost powerless to prevent songs being passed around for free on the internet. Very often fans would have the records long before they were released in shops.

In 1996, when the first demos from Olympic Studios were leaked on to fansites, there was some alarm among the band and label but they soon realised that it was just a sign of interest in the record. But, in the years since then, labels had become increasingly scared of such leaks. It was becoming more and more difficult to make money out of record sales.

When The Verve signed to EMI again, they were joining a record label that seemed, at times, to be in a state of panic. Many big names were starting to wonder whether record labels were worth the vast sums of money they took from every album sold. At the beginning of 2008, Robbie Williams' manager released a statement saying that he would be refusing to give the company his new album unless he received assurances as to how it would be marketed.

"The question is," he said to *The Times*, "should Robbie deliver the new album he is due to release to EMI? We have to say the answer is no. We have no idea how EMI will market and promote the album. They do not have anyone in the digital sphere capable of doing the job required."

At around the same time, it was reported that Paul McCartney had accused EMI of being "boring" and of having little idea how to market him. After a 44-year association with the company, he left them and signed a deal with Starbucks' musical division Hear Music.

Even more innovatively, Radiohead abandoned the standard industry route all together, putting out their 2007 album *In Rainbows* themselves and making it available on a pay-what-you-like basis online. Thom Yorke said that their record label's new management, venture capital company Terra Firma, were acting like a "confused bull in a china shop."

In this climate, The Verve, or at least manager Jazz Summers, were unlikely to have much confidence in their label. Not surprisingly, following further worrying comments from the top names at EMI, Summers grasped the nettle. Not long afterwards it was reported in *The Daily Telegraph* that Jazz was considering taking action. "The Verve are to join Robbie Williams and Coldplay in threatening to withhold their next album from EMI until they receive assurances about marketing and the company's financial health," they said. "Why would we deliver a record when EMI is cutting back on the marketing and is in financial difficulty?" Jazz was quoted.

This might just have been a negotiating tactic. When Jazz Summers went to discuss the advance for The Verve's fourth album he, according to industry rumour, took in the sales figures of *Urban Hymns* as a starting point. EMI then, allegedly, suggested that they take the sales figures of the last Richard Ashcroft solo album as a starting point.

But in an industry that was changing on a daily basis, it was hard for anybody to know how well an album would do, regardless of the marketing muscle behind it or the 'brand name'. That depended on The Verve themselves. The truth was nobody knew what they would come up with next. Even their two biggest hits, 'Bitter Sweet Symphony' and 'The Drugs Don't Work', sounded nothing like each other.

The way The Verve operate just doesn't fit neatly into a marketing plan. To market a band successfully it's helpful to know that they will appeal to roughly the same people with every album. This implies making roughly the same kind of music every time but The Verve had never done that. Nick would rarely even play the same way twice in one recording session, let alone over several years!

This meant that at the start of 2008, there were two groups of people desperately wishing for a particular version of The Verve to re-emerge. The first were the executives of Terra Firma, who must have been praying every day for another global smash along the lines of 'Bitter Sweet Symphony' or 'The Drugs Don't Work'.

The other group were the bloggers and the fanzine writers, hoping that they would come back with more fifteen minute epics of maniacal space-rock. Before their first shows, it would have been easy for the casual observer to believe that, on the fringes of the internet, at least, songs like 'All In The Mind' were just as well known as 'Lucky Man' or 'Sonnet'. The best way for Verve fans to prove they were true believers was to hail those early tracks and sniffily dismiss *Urban Hymns* as the moment when things went wrong.

'The Thaw Sessions' suggested that the band themselves were closer to the second camp, which must have worried EMI. Then again, some of the live reviews of their comeback shows posted an alternative reality where The Verve, instead of becoming soul-baring pop stars, had travelled down the route of 'This Is Music' and become something closer to a modern Led Zeppelin.

When they went into the State Of The Ark studio in 2007, they could do anything they wanted but the question was: would they all want the same thing? Did they still have the desire to be the biggest band in the world? After rising from the dead twice, nobody would dare predict that The Verve didn't have it in them to finally fulfil their potential. Unlike so many guitar bands of their era, they'd never settled for merely rehashing the best bits of rock 'n' roll history. Richard was once asked in a 1997 TV interview about his frequent claim that they were the best band in the world.

"All we're saying is, rock 'n' roll wise, we're the best band in the world," he replied. "That's not to say that people in the dance community aren't making incredible music, that people in the hip-hop community aren't making incredible music. It's just that rock 'n' roll is such an old hag, an old corpse, that anybody who can breathe some life into it must be doing something great because it's been raped and pillaged for 30 years."

By the end of the 20th Century, very few bands had the attitude that it was possible to create something new out of rock 'n' roll. The Verve's lack of reverence for the past was just one of the things that made them special. They'd arrived in a time when rock seemed, to many people, like a relic of the past. Even when Britpop came along and made being retro acceptable, they still sounded fresh and modern. And that was why, in the middle of 2008, it was so good to have them back – whatever they've decided to do.

The Verve stand comparison with the other great survivors of the early Nineties, Radiohead and Blur, for the way that they reinvented themselves. Even now there are relatively few people who love every second of The Verve's recorded output, from their deep space beginnings with 'A Man Called Sun' to 'Sonnet' or 'Lucky Man'.

Perhaps only Richard Ashcroft really appreciates both those two extremes of music equally.

Although many great bands emerged in the Nineties, not least the two just mentioned, very few combined that spirit of adventure and innovation with Ashcroft's genuine star quality. That's what made him interesting even when the records he was making weren't quite up to The Verve's standards. He, paradoxically, combines incredible self-belief with a spark of self-doubt that has led him constantly to try and better himself.

He could have just pushed The Verve around the world for ten years, churning out slightly different versions of 'The Drugs Don't Work' and replacing members as they fell away. He could have launched their comeback tour by simply raking in the cash with a run-through of the Greatest Hits. That he didn't do either means, very probably, that he'll make more great music as well as more mistakes and say more ridiculous things as well as affect more lives in the future.

One thing is certain, the volatility of the band's chemistry remains – even at the time of writing there are rumours circulating that inter-band tensions are again running high. Perhaps another 'split' might happen, perhaps not. The Verve might well break-up again in another burst of acrimony but there will always be that spirit of *adventure*.

One of Richard Ashcroft's greatest talents is getting the best out of the people around him. He was the one who drove The Verve to the top – but they were the engine and the wheels. No doubt he'll record more solo albums and work with other people in the future but it is The Verve, perhaps more than any other element of his career, that has fulfilled his childhood dreams. As an eighteen year old, when he sat on the hill above Wigan and looked down at the lights below, what he visualised was probably stardom, pure and simple; by 2008, stardom meant little to him. What matters is the music. The music that is behind him and, more importantly, the music that is still to come.

ALSO
AVAILABLE

FROM

INDEPENDENT MUSIC PRESS

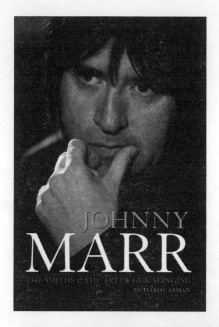

JOHNNY MARR: THE SMITHS & THE ART OF GUN-SLINGING
by Richard Carman

The Smiths were the best British band since The Beatles. Their shimmering, muscular, guitar-driven pop remains the barometer for everyone who looks back at the 1980s with affection. In a decade that arguably produced more poor pop music than any other since the 1950s, The Smiths shone like a beacon and inspired a generation of indie guitar bands, and their influence continues undiminished to this day. After The Smiths, Marr continued to inject beautiful, sophisticated guitar into some of the best music of the period: The Pretenders, Kirsty McColl, Billy Bragg, The The and Talking Heads all benefited from his incendiary input. More recently with his band Johnny Marr & The Healers,Johnny remains as influential and important as ever. This is the first full-length biography of Johnny Marr, looking beyond world of The Smiths and into the solo career of Britain's most influential guitar player of the last two decades – a tale coloured by exclusive interviews with people such as key Smiths insider Grant Showbiz, Billy Bragg and David Byrne. A must-read for anyone who cares about The Smiths as well as great rock or pop.

ISBN 0 9549704 8 9 208 Pages Paperback, 8pp b/w pics £12.99 World Rights

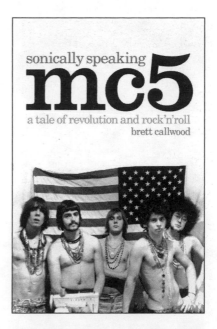

MC5: SONICALLY SPEAKING – A TALE OF PUNK ROCK AND REVOLUTION
by Brett Callwood

The first in-depth biography of the group, Sonically Speaking charts the career of this most seminal of bands, as well as unravelling what became of the members after the break up of the MC5. For this definitive book, author Brett Callwood travelled to Detroit and Los Angeles to track down and interview the three surviving founder members of the MC5 in-depth. He also spoke at length with other key players in this remarkable tale, such as former manager John Sinclair, artist Gary Grimshaw, former White Panther Pun Plamondon, Leni Sinclair, Jackson Smith – the son that MC5's Fred had with Patti Smith – and Russ Gibb, manager of the legendary Grandee Ballroom, among others.

ISBN 0 9552822-2-5 224 Pages Paperback, 12 b/w pics £12.99 World Rights

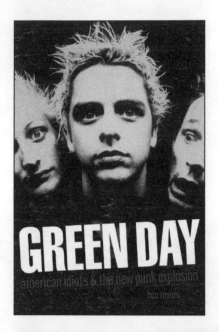

GREEN DAY: AMERICAN IDIOTS AND THE NEW PUNK EXPLOSION
by Ben Myers

The world's first and only full biography of Green Day. Self-confessed latch-key kids from small blue-collar Californian towns, Green Day have gone on to sell 50 million albums and single-handedly redefine the punk and rock genre for an entire generation. Inspired by both the energy of British punk bands as well as cult American groups, Green Day gigged relentlessly across the US underground before eventually signing to Warners and releasing their 1994 major label debut *Dookie*, which was a 10-million-selling worldwide hit album. With the arrival of Green Day, suddenly music was dumb, fun, upbeat and colourful again. Many now credit the band with saving rock from the hands of a hundred grunge-lite acts. In 2004 Green Day reached a career pinnacle with the concept album *American Idiot*, a sophisticated commentary on modern life - not least their dissatisfaction with their president. Myers is an authority on punk and hardcore and in this unauthorised book charts the band members' difficult childhoods and their rise to success, speaking to key members of the punk underground and music industry figures along the way.

ISBN 0 9539942 9 5 208 Pages Paperback, 8pp b/w pics £12.99 World Rights

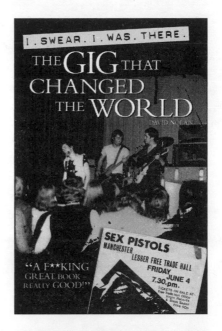

I SWEAR I WAS THERE: THE GIG THAT CHANGED THE WORLD

by David Nolan

On June 4, 1976, four young men took the stage of a tiny upstairs hall in Manchester for a gig that, quite literally, *changed the world*. In front of a handful of people they played one of the most important live sets of all time. Alongside Woodstock and Live Aid, the Sex Pistols performance at the Lesser Free Trade Hall has been named by critics as one of the most pivotal performances in music history ... not necessarily because of the quality of the music – but because of the effect the music had on the audience.

Members of Joy Division and New Order, the Smiths, the Fall and Buzzcocks were there that night as well as Tony Wilson. The truth behind that gig – plus the Pistols repeat performance six weeks later and their first ever TV appearance – has been shrouded in mystery for thirty years. Until now, everyone's been happy to print the legend. For the first time, here's the truth. Featuring previously unpublished photos and interviews with key players and audience members.

ISBN 0 9549704 9 7 208 Pages Paperback, 40 b/w pics £12.99 World Rights

Visit our website at www.impbooks.com for more
information on our full list of titles including books on:

Bernard Sumner, MC5, Bruce Dickinson, Robert Plant,
Slash, 'Skins', 'Scooter Boys', Dave Grohl, Muse, The Streets,
Kasabian, Green Day, Ian Hunter, Mick Ronson,
David Bowie, The Killers, My Chemical Romance,
System Of A Down, The Prodigy and many more.

www.myspace.com/independentmusicpress